The Legend That Was CLAPHAM

All good things...

Gloucester Cathedral as seen from Priory Road.

The Legend That Was CLAPHAM

All Good Things...

by

Donald Bullock

Published by The Wheatley Press
Innsworth Technology Park, D5
Innsworth Lane
Gloucester, GL3 1DL
England.

www.wheatleypress.com

First edition published
Autumn 2002

Second edition published
Spring 2012

Published by The Wheatley Press
Innsworth Technology Park, D5
Innsworth Lane
Gloucester, GL3 1DL
England.

www.wheatleypress.com

ISBN 978-0954195809

This book is dedicated to those who were part of the legend that was Clapham. Both the living and the dead.

In The Legend That Was Clapham, Donald Bullock gathers his boyhood memories and household gleanings of Clapham, the parish of his birth in the early 'Thirties.

Some of the happenings portrayed in this book were originally published as magazine articles in the mid-eighties, whilst other fragments have been extracted from the manuscript of his forthcoming book Hovels and Haydust, and endowed with greater local detail.

'Hovels and Haydust', the author's complete boyhood autobiography of his life in the parochial Gloucester of the 'Thirties, with its then tiny, earthy and bustling market town, its rolling countryside of family farms, its meadows rich with colourful wild flowers and chirping insect life, and its wealth of rivers, streams and pools, is considerably wider ranging. It is due for publication by The Wheatley Press in the near future.

Contents

Illustrations

Photographs marked thus* were conceived and taken by the author in the 'Eighties for a series of illustrated magazine articles and posed by authentically dressed models in, wherever possible, the original settings.

Foreword

Donald Bullock was born in Clapham's Alvin Street on Barton Fair Day in 1932, over Bill Keeling's newsagent's shop, where his parents lived in a rented room. The first of their five children, he attended Kingsholm Infants' School and Oakbank Open Air School, then the notoriously Dickensian National School in Gloucester's London Road, before moving on to the Gloucester Central School for Boys.

Mercifully, he says, there was then no such thing as television, and he and his peers spent their unshackled and crowded outdoor lives both in the earthy market-town centre and about the hills and vales, rivers, streams and pools of its surrounding countryside.

As he has written elsewhere in his captivating prose: 'We were an energetic set, and every dawning day came packed with adventure, much of it money-making. We roamed errands about the town, mingled and earned in the city centre cattle and fruit markets, carried parcels at the stations, searched and climbed for birds' eggs, (a normal boyhood pursuit in those days) and picked colourful wild flowers by the armful from the roadside verges and meadows.'

They gathered wild strawberries in Newent woods, mushrooms in Maisemore; picked blackberries, caught rabbits and slept out in makeshift tents on Chosen hill to music from their home-made crystal sets, and, in winter, gathered and sold holly and mistletoe, bundled and sold firewood and undertook snow-clearing for their neighbours. They went pike fishing on the river Leadon and at the Walham and Ashleworth pools, where they sometimes had to break the ice first, and, as Christmas approached, went carol-singing in the evenings.

He and his peers knew every inch of the Nunnies – 'that adventurous stream of secret worlds, bounded by its willow-draped sage greenery, that slid and babbled between the Cheltenham and Tewkesbury Roads and on to the river...' and, like his peers, he both caught many a redbreast and suffered many a 'bootful' in his years of 'bamping' there.

What coppers came their way had to be earned, and they spent them frugally. They made their own fishing rods and tackle and became experts at fishing every nook of all the local waters: the Leadon, the Severn and its plethora of streams and riverside pools, and both the Gloucester and Stroud canals. He can still make a professional-looking float in a minute with a pigeon quill, a razor blade and a dip of crimson nail varnish...

An ancient and upright bike occasionally came their way, and they used it energetically to broaden their horizons. One pedalled, one sat on the crossbar and the other ran alongside, often to Highnam, Minsterworth or the Lassington or Newent woods, sometimes further, taking it in turns to pedal, sit or run.

After leaving school he worked in The Gloucester Citizen's photographic department where he spent, he says, the happiest and most interesting few years of his life, until he was forced by family circumstances to leave his haven for a series of better paid but sadly cramping jobs.

He duly became busily self-employed but found time, over the years, to write for many publications, and he remains regularly published today.

Now retired, he is working on the completion of 'Hovels and Haydust', his moving, eye-opening, sometimes tragic and often hilarious account of a boy's childhood in and around a Gloucester long since gone forever. He has never, he says, known boredom, and vigorously recalls his boyhood days as though they were of yesterday.

Author's Note

As the 'Thirties dawned I was born into the parish of Clapham, as had been many of my family, and although my people were to move house often, I grew up steeped in its society, its streets, its shops, and its characters. It was an invigorating place, Clapham, and, with its wonderful and embracing culture, delightfully and earthily unique.

In the nineteen-eighties' I wove some of my memories into a commissioned series of purpose-illustrated articles for a country magazine, and one of these, upon Clapham and its folk, evoked widespread interest and many letters. When I later came to write the 'Clapham' chapter for my boyhood autobiography Hovels and Haydust I increasingly felt that the conception, life and wanton destruction of Clapham justified a book of its own.

The result, offered here, is a much expanded and researched version of that chapter with an added blend of historical facts and photographs, a wealth of other people's memories and my own childhood recollections of the Clapham culture into which I was born. I hope that in some small measure the whole might help to keep its memory alive.

One final word. After so many years, memories can play tricks. There may be mistakes or omissions. I would be grateful to hear from anyone with constructive comments, information or photographs, so that in the event of a further edition the book might be improved.

Donald Bullock, Spring 2012.

donald@wheatleypress.com

Donald Bullock in 1937

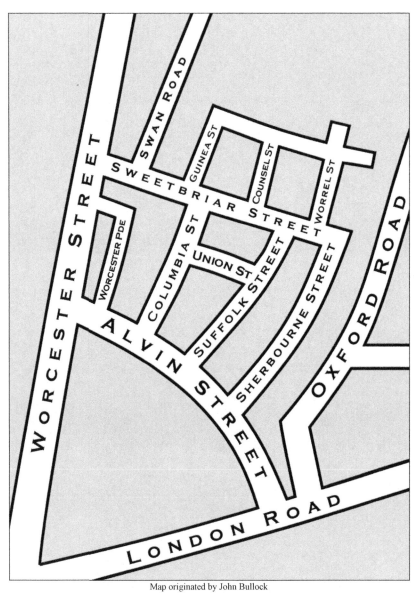

Map originated by John Bullock

George Worrall Counsel's concept of Clapham

Acknowledgements

I would like to acknowledge those who have helped me, in their various ways, with the production of this book; in particular, the following:

To the staff of the Gloucester City Library and of the Gloucestershire Record Office, who dipped into their treasures and brought many useful items of information and detail to my attention.

The late Charlie Whitfield, of The Jolly Waterman, the former riverside pub on the banks of the Severn at Walham, for the many hours of golden riverside yarns and memories so enthusiastically imparted during my fishing spells on the river and at Walham Brickpits. To have known Charlie, and to have enjoyed his modest and authentic riverside facts and stories, delivered in his rich and balanced Gloucester accent, was a bounty in itself. And to his son Jim, also a recognised Severn authority, for the rich gems of riverside information imparted, and for the loan of Charlie's photograph.

The late Jim Clements, of Sandhurst, Gloucester, that sadly-missed mine of wisdom and knowledge of old Gloucester and a dear friend, for his many factual and detailed letters over the years, and for the hours of invigorating recollections imparted to me both at his local, The Globe, and at his home, who ought to have taken the advice of his friends and written a book of his own, and who would have done so very much better. And to his gracious widow Molly for her continued interest in my project and for the loan of Jim's photograph.

The well-known L.E. 'Peter' Copeland of Churchdown, whom I recall as so busily and expertly photographing the 'Thirties Gloucester (including our hovel of the day) and John Rowden of Hempsted, also no mean cameraman, both of whom received me so courteously at their homes during the preparation of this book and both of whom so readily gave me permission to use their excellent photographs.

The late Mrs Betty Dix – whom, as lads we knew as Betty Redburn of Bet's Wonder Stores in the heart of Clapham, for checking sections of my manuscript, for providing valued photographs, and for imparting her vintage Clapham memories to me whilst I was writing in Spain, and who so sadly and suddenly died as I arrived in Gloucester to renew our acquaintanceship.

To the many Gloucester characters who, on their journeys through their lives and mine, advertised their rich and differing formulas for coping with the adversities dealt with their poverty. And to the folks of Clapham; those who remain, and those who are no more. I hope this book does something to preserve the memories of their wonderful way of life, the like of which we shall not see again.

And finally, to those who lent their practical help. To my son John, who brought his immense computer skills to the production of the book's illustrations, often from ancient and damaged originals, and who originated its cover, and to my son James, who set out the manuscript and combined it with John's computer images to produce the original facsimile of this book.

And to my wife Jeannette, for so ably helping me in my research, and for so patiently accompanying me along the memories of ancient and winding byways we never knew together.

I am grateful to them all.

Chapter 1

The Dawning of a Dream

The parish of Clapham, alas, is no more, yet almost half a century after its senseless destruction, the rhythm of its name still breathes its magic about the streets of Gloucester.

Why is Clapham such a legend? What was Clapham in its heyday?

To those merely concerned with its geography, Clapham was an embracing term for an expansive huddle of city centre backstreets towards the northern side of the Gloucester Bowl, but to those who knew its magic, and perhaps lived there and shared its soul, Clapham was a friendly haven with sturdy roots, an old-established and self-contained community with a fiercely beating heart of its own.

Its concept began in the early eighteen twenties, and an examination of the Gloucester civic scene of the day strongly suggests that it might well have been the brainchild of a truly remarkable and well respected local light, George Worrall Counsel, who was born in the 1750's. Whilst there seems little concrete proof of this, I have heard of no other name arising for the credit, and I think it appropriate that students of Clapham's origin – as well as those at all interested in the recent history of Gloucester - would do well to learn something of him. It should be remembered that the Gloucester of his early days was a tiny and medieval place with a population of some seven thousand, and the gates which for centuries had risen in its walls were still intact. Its East gate remained until 1780, its North and South gates stood a while longer, and its West gate remained in place until 1809.

George Worrall Counsel

George Worrall Counsel (1758–1843) was the son of Joshua Counsel, an eminent Gloucester surgeon. He was born in the local parish of Holy Trinity on the 6th of July 1758, and received a classical education at the King's school.

He was an extremely intelligent student with a highly retentive memory whose delights included the study of the arts and sciences and general literature. Upon leaving school he was apprenticed to an ironmonger - a lucrative business in those days – until a friend of his one day called into the Westgate Street shop where he worked and chastised him for wasting his time. 'With your education and abilities you should be in one of the learned professions, Master George, not stuck here selling tin-tacks!' he scolded, and after soberly reflecting upon this advice George left the ironmongers and went to study law.

He swiftly rose to become an attorney-at-law and a proctor. His interests also extended to local antiquarian lore and he soon became noted as an authority in these fields. Nobody, it was said, would think of covering up a newly discovered mosaic pavement, or disposing of an item of pottery, or a newly discovered old coin, without first referring it to him for his findings. His elegantly written papers on his discoveries were published both in the intellectual journals of the day and in the local papers, and the people of Gloucester came to regard him as the custodian of their local history.

With his mild and unruffled temper and mild disposition he was widely regarded as being a delightful and intellectual companion. He had a full measure of wisdom, a wide vocabulary, a pleasing speaking voice, and an excellent sense of witty and innocent humour. He delighted in lampooning his fellow councillors and others in doggerel verse.

He became, during his eighty-five year span, very well-connected, numbering many eminent people among his friends. One was his old school friend Jemmy Wood, the well-known and affluent Gloucester banker and miser, who left him £10,000 in his will, and others included the respected fellow antiquarian and top publisher of the day T.D. Fossebroke, whom he assisted in the writing of the celebrated History and Antiquities of Gloucester. In 1829 he became an author in his own right when he published his

History of the City of Gloucester, and in 1841 he wrote and published The Life and Martyrdom of Bishop Hooper. He continued to practise as an attorney and proctor until he was 81. After his death in his 85th year, on January 19th, 1843, some of his papers were sold to Sir Thomas Phillipps, and some 160 items were later sold by Sotheby's.

Counsel was a far-seeing man who was more conscious than his forerunners of current and recent events, and it seems likely that by the 1820's, when major rail, road and canal links came to exploit Gloucester's strategically important and favourable geographical position, he would have anticipated the nature of the phenomenal local changes due to come about.

Industrialisation was about to reach the hitherto parochial Gloucester, and its population was set to explode. The incoming workers, who would be drawn mainly from the west midlands, would need houses to live in, and his answer to that lay in the design and construction of a large and entirely new parish of simple artisans' dwellings on Monkleighton Grounds, a central expanse of land Counsel owned, and after the laying of its plans, its building commenced in 1822.

When it was completed, the following decade, the new parish of Clapham consisted of a network of compact brick-built terrace houses set within a total of ten streets, and it is interesting to note that two of these – Worrall Street and Counsel Street - were named after Counsel. The whole locality occupied an area between London Road and Worcester Street, and was flanked on its south-western side by Alvin Street. In the absence of any other likely candidate for the conception and realisation of the parish of Clapham, it seems reasonable that the honour should be accorded to George Worrall Counsel, and I have allowed myself this assumption in these pages.

Clapham in the Nineteen Thirties

North of the new Sweetbriar Street, which ran through its northern side, was a large expanse of land known as the 'Rec'.

This once fine recreation ground had slipped to lumpy wasteland by the Nineteen Thirties, though I recall a set or two of ancient iron swings and a row of tiny, open-topped and door-less privy cubicles, each separated from its neighbour by a heavy slate sheet. Nearby lay the ruins of the old Barron's foundry.

The local lads of the day built their summer dens on the Rec, and camped overnight in them when the weather bloomed. It was also the venue of the men-folks' Sunday morning pitch and toss schools, which were run by one 'Rod', or Rodney. They were good-natured affairs, these, and many's the time I saw a winner read sadness in the face of a loser and slip him a coin or two of his winnings. Such gambling was frowned upon, of course, so the players routinely stationed 'look-outs' about, but for the most part they need scarcely have bothered. The police knew all about it and apart from the odd token 'sortie' they left them in their peace, though one amusing incident was related to me by Stan Green, a former Clapham lad and no mean Clapham authority. It concerned a well-known offender who, anxious to escape a zealous policeman's pursuit one Sunday morning, surprised a family at the far end of his terrace row by dashing uninvited through their front door, running up their stairs and scrambling into their loft, so enabling him to travel along the continuous corridor of roof space to the refuge of his own home. But generally, like the rest of the city authorities the police respected the people of Clapham, who were self-sufficient and undemanding as well as essentially law-abiding.

I never saw a policeman in Clapham, nor knew any locked doors. A few folks were known for their pugilistic tendencies when fired by their Saturday night drink, but their animosities faded as their demons slipped away. There were the odd scamps about, too, but their craftiness was petty and transparent. They were invariably local characters with an amusement value and most were held in grudging affection.

The Dwellings

Clapham's dwellings were all much alike, having a living room and stone-floored kitchen, a tacked-on coalhouse, and two bedrooms. Most were simply furnished and heavily-draped against the winter cold and their society's sounds of living.

The living room had an iron grate whose black-leading was one of life's chores. Every family burned coal, and most cooked over their fires as well. Each living-room mantelpiece was graced by a single gaslight, and when its glow began to dim its redemption came with a penny fed to its meter. None of the houses had a bathroom. The privy was a shanty hut with a latched board-door at the far end of the yard, and I knew no family that aspired to toilet paper. Folks used newspaper instead. This was often torn into neat squares, threaded onto a loop of string and hung on a nail, and those who lingered 'up the back' were usually having a leisurely and peaceful read.

Some dwellings were built in clusters around tiny communal courtyards with an unroofed privy and a tap over a yellow clay sink. The yards were accessed by alleys or covered passages set into the terrace rows, and these came named after their erstwhile occupants. I recall Woods' and Andersons' Passage, and others named after the Coopers, the Smiths' and the Carrington-Windos'.

Clapham's community was served by an ornate church and a strict and effective school, both of which were named after St. Mark, and by numerous little shops, many of which were in the front rooms of their proprietors.

Our Room over Keelings'

Bill and Gladys Keeling occupied a paper-shop on the corner of Alvin Street and Sherbourne Street. My people rented an upstairs room from them and it was there, on Barton Fair Day in the dawning 'Thirties that I first saw the light of day.

With my coming they aspired to a place of their own, my people, and eventually they found a tiny cottage nearby. Time came to move there, and they piled their bits onto a borrowed handcart, put me in my old mahogany drawer (they hadn't yet run to a cot or 'pram), put that on the handcart, and carted me there too. And it was there, in the very Bowl of Gloucester that my yesterdays faded and my dawning came to me.

Playing in the Streets

Whilst a sprinkling of children played in the Rec, the most popular playgrounds were the streets, which rang noisily to their variety of games.

The boys and girls formed two separate societies. The boys typically played football, using almost anything for a ball and their coats for goalpost markers, or they played improvised cricket, usually with an old tennis ball and with their stumps chalked on the walls. Others played marbles along the gutters, and a few struggled with primitive and well-worn roller skates strung all too loosely to their boots. They played cannon and rounders, too, and in autumn the streets rang to their conker games with their axiomatic bickerings.

"Bags tangles! Free go!"

"You tangled 'im a-purpose..."

"I never!"

"You did!"

"That ent never the 'undred and fiver you 'ad yes'ty..."

"Il is! I betcha! Ask our kid!!"

"That conker o' yourn's a baked 'un. Baked 'uns an' last year's 'uns ent allowed..."

The girls were gentler, of course. They hung in their gossiping groups, or chanted their rhymes, or tucked their frocks into their knickers to play their skipping games, or hopscotch on their chalked squares. And one or two of the more adventurous swung happily if clumsily on ropes hoisted to the gas lamp posts by the boys. And all came lost in their play whilst the occasional trundling car deferred to them, for the streets had forever been the children's playgrounds, and the grown-ups who sailed their chariots there acknowledged their intrusion.

Fanny Thesp

Sometimes a girl from the neighbouring Knapp - if Fanny Thesp could be called a girl - would slope over to intrude into the girls' games. Fanny was a maiden of qualities - of a sort. She seemed a perpetual and childish seventeen, though not a very sweet seventeen, being huge, slow and slothful, and none too refined or respectful. She wore white ankle socks and flat shoes and her discordant nasal speech knew no niceties. She belched publicly for pleasure, always needed a hanky but never had one, and was publicly and joyfully flatulent.

She nursed a compulsion for conversational intrusion and an affinity for personal trivia, and could devastate an objector with a single foul word. She nurtured a love of pavement hopscotch, too, and entered every game she saw as of right.

Her intrusions brought confusions, delays and difficulties, but they were tolerated by those who knew her, and those who didn't soon found why, for at the first sign of their distaste Fanny would bestow them a basic descriptive noun and up and cuff them. It would be a clumsy swing. Just one. It was enough.

Robinswood Hill & Wainlodes

On Sunday afternoons in summer many of Clapham's young pulled a sandwich or two together, scooped up a bottle of water or pop, and somehow collared pushbikes for getting out of Clapham. They travelled the highway in their droves, and an arbitrary picture they made, for the bikes they rode rarely fitted them. There'd be tall ones on small bikes, peddling on their heels with their toes askew, short ones on tall bikes, unable to reach the saddles, girls on mens' bikes with one leg pedalling through the frame, and boys upright and ajerk on their mothers' sit-up-and-beg bikes with the saddles stabbing at their backs...

Often they'd make for Robinswood Hill, but when the weather ran really warm most would court the river; and off they'd straggle, along the Tewkesbury Road and into the narrow, winding and leafy lanes of Norton, to climb themselves to the brow of Wainlodes Hill with its still delightful panoramic view of the wide pastoral green beside the Severn and its vales.

And there, having all but arrived, they'd stop, as I so often did, to find their breath, to savour the view, and to joyfully anticipate the dangerous thrill that was to come. Then they'd loosen their brakes and allow the pitch, the steepest they knew, to sail them down the slope at speed, past the Red Lion at the bottom and to the spacious and grassy banks where the slow and lazy brown river curved and fattened and sidled past the inn and round the sunken barges and on towards the cliffs.

And there they'd stop, that happy and contented clan, to sit with the sun and while away their time with their sandwiches and drinks, whilst some plied a willow stick and line to the river, others paddled in the shallows and the more daring ignored the river-planted warning signs and swam.

And there they'd nestle to while away their bliss until, all too soon, the sun slipped large and low and red over the meadows with their peacefully grazing cows. And with their faces glowing in its gold they'd struggle and coax their bikes back up the hill, climb aboard them at its brow, and sail off to their roots again.

Clapham's Lives

Clapham, when I came to it in the 'Thirties, hosted a warm and caring culture whose folks knew great humanity but few skills, and with manual workers in perpetual abundance, unemployment and poverty had reigned endemic for generations. The resultant prolonged hardships had bred a tough, resilient and delightfully unspoiled people of character, dependability and neighbourliness. There was no conception of the welfare state to come, and wearing life's unfairnesses like garlands they relished and savoured their good times and supported each other in their times of need.

They were straight, direct and uncomplicated, the folks of Clapham, easy to get on with and slow to complain. Theirs was a culture not of material advancement, but of communal spirit. Few thought much of their tomorrows, or of seeking to gain at another's expense, and getting themselves and their clan through each successive day was about the limit of their aspirations. Nor did many stray far, for Clapham was their own integrated society with its uniquely supportive culture.

There were, of course, those who couldn't aspire to a proper job because of bad health or enforced family ties. The burdens and premature deaths caused by the likes of diphtheria and consumption saw to that. Yet most found their ways of keeping a place, and their enterprises welled from necessity. Some begged or borrowed handcarts and ran portering. Others developed knacks into marketable skills. 'Leaky' Smith was good with dripping taps; Art' Hall tinkered tunes out of tired wireless sets, and we ran our leaking bowls and baths to Perc' Young. And Charlie South was good with bikes; he kept a pump down his sock and lumped his waistcoat with valves and patches. He could hear and mend a puncture in a minute, and bend your spoons and forks for nothing. And, it might as well be said, Tod Fisher was a bookie that could run.

Backyard Fowls

Clapham's dawns came heralded with the trumpeting calls of its cockerels, for about half of its backyards housed a shanty run of fowls together with a cockerel. The fowls were kept for their eggs, some of which were preserved in waterglass for the winter, and the cockerel would meet its demise as Christmas came. It was common to hear, from across the yards, the cries and commotions of a doomed bird at the hands of its untaught slayers. The women at their windows would gather their little ones and finger their chins and fret, but once the bird had lost, it was all soon forgotten. Times were hard and folks' sensitivities didn't stretch much past their clan and its daily needs.

Apart from those who kept a Christmas cockerel, Clapham folk scarcely knew the luxury of its taste. The most they would aspire to at Christmas would be a joint of pork. And we never knew anyone who'd tasted turkey.

'Bad Women'

Clapham nursed few secrets. Everyone knew everybody's business and they generally judged each other with understanding. But because they were a moral lot, one class of person was abhorred, and this was, in the saying of the day, the woman reckoned to be 'no better than she should be'. One lived close to us, and although she was open and friendly to all, she was universally despised and discredited, even by those who scarcely knew her, and her life came blighted by the incessantly hostile gossip.

Sundays

Sundays were days of restraint, and Clapham, like the rest of the Bowl, fell silent, for these were cloistered times. Everybody wore their Sunday best except the very poorest, who settled for brushing their clothes with a dry scrubbing brush, polishing their shoes, and combing their hair with water. The core of its society attended St. Mark's Church and most of the children were sent to Sunday school. Even those with scant time for religion respected the cloth. Blasphemy was avoided as lowering and potentially retributive and any mildly derogatory oath or remark would be answered with a murmured reprimand, even from hardy agnostics. Family attendance at the church was considered mandatory, not only for Christenings, marriages and deaths, but for harvest festivals and church and Sunday school anniversaries.

The vicar of St. Mark's for the first twenty years of my life was the Reverend Robert Harwood. An utterly genuine and good man with an exceptionally sunny and delightful outlook, he was forever on his feet around the streets in his swirling black cloak, and was highly respected and revered by every Clapham soul. The people of his parish were his life, and he had the gift of divining unhappiness or need, however well it was hidden, and answering it in the person's home with both comfort and practical help, whether the person was a church-goer or not. His church was Clapham's heart and soul, and was crowded every Sunday.

Spotless Homes

Clapham's housewives were a practical and unpretentious lot. They kept their terrace homes spotless, and extended their fussiness beyond their front doors. Having seen their charges off to work or school, they'd pop out and polish their brass doorknobs and knockers, wipe off their front window sills, shine up their windows and sweep the length of their fronts. Then they'd disappear inside to do their housework.

Then, around mid-morning, their front doors would fly open and we'd see their pinafored forms scrubbing their bleached-white wooden doorsteps and washing their patch of pavement to a neat and darkened semi-circle. Then they'd slip inside again, to cook the family dinner.

Flies

But even the house-proud could do little about the proliferation of flies. They came in their gangs as the days ran warm and joined us as we ate; they ran on our sugar, sucked at our butter, played in our hair and trifled with our tempers. We knew no sprays then, but sometimes, when the pestering came too much, we boys would be put to attacking them with rolled-up newspapers until we'd flattened every one. But our peace would be short-lived. We'd soon notice one circling in the air, then another, and before long we'd have a houseful again.

One day our mother brought a flypaper home and hung it from the ceiling. It was the first I'd seen, a spiralling band of lethal syrup weighted by its bottle-green case.

11

"Here, watch that for a few minutes, Donnie." she said. "See if it clears the room of these dratted flies." And she went bumbling about her work.

I pounced into a chair and studied the glossy strip, then moved my gaze to the flies soaring and banking around it. After a while one landed on it and struggled and stuck. So did another, and another. It was a silent and effective trap, and I joyfully willed its victims towards it and watched with sadistic joy as they wove their ways to their doom. Before long a battalion of fastened flies were struggling for their lives, and although one or two pulled free to retire to their final arsenical ablutions, the rest were held fast and their antics glued them faster, until wearied by their threshing they sank and perished whilst their peers circled placidly about them.

It wasn't long before that paper wore a garment of flies, and as I watched them in their final moments, my satisfaction gave way to a moment's reflection. We were killing them because they bothered us, because they were flies. It was the same with the local rats, and the carcases in the butchers' sheds. They all paid the price of being what they were, because that was their lot. There was no underlying fairness.

Anyway, in spite of our efforts, the flies' endlessly gyrating numbers never fell. Our remedies seemed to summon their reserves, and that, it seemed, was *our* lot. We had flies, or we had flypapers and flies...

<u>Modern Times...</u>

These were the days of carts and drays. Their horses were everywhere, and every street breathed their flavour as they brought the pubs their beer, the shopkeepers' their supplies, and delivered their milk and bread and coal around the doors. And they brought a bonus to some. Those with a patch of garden kept a bucket and shovel to hand, and would run out with them when the opportunity arose.

But cars were chugging at the roads, too. Many were huge and ornate chariots, strangely without their horses, and with running boards to fit a family. Then Henry Ford took a hand, and made some smaller. 'Any colour as long as it's black.' he announced, and black they were. And, so it was said, cheap. But cars didn't come our way much, and we never knew anybody who'd been in one, much less owned one. A few came rattling along Worcester Street, though the horses and wagons and the barrows and handcarts curbed their speed. And they often seemed to wheeze and boil. We'd see them at the roadside with their bonnets up and their owners peering beneath them, and those who came to help them sometimes came by horse and cart.

And machines came spluttering to the air, too, often trailing their streamers. We'd hear a chugging and a popping and look up to see the futuristic silver emblem fighting the clouds with no apparent means of support, and the older folks would fly to their doorways, or nestle beneath their eaves, and steal dark looks to the skies as they scowled and shook their heads.

"'Tain't natural." they'd mutter. "'Tain't right, neither. There's no reason to 'em, and no soul to 'em. An' them as don't drop on us'll poison the sky and turn the weather. They'll do for us all afore they finish. Ther's nothin' more certain. Just you wait an' see..."

Chapter 2

The Shops

Clapham's shops were a mixed lot. No two were alike, but they were all Dickensian and many of the interiors had been pulled together with whatever was to hand. None was grand and none I knew was even slightly pretentious. Some had simple wooden counters, others had home-made structures of bits of board, and a few had just a table. Most were a workaday shambles, and like the rest of Clapham they all glowed by golden gaslight after dark. Most shopkeepers kept a thick (and often greasy) credit ledger wherein they dotted their customers' debts with their freshly licked indelible pencils. With money tight and credit universal, keeping a Clapham shop that paid was a tongue-purpling business.

Alvin Street was Clapham's main thoroughfare, and its variety of little shops hung roughly in two clusters, one nearest its London Road end and the other closest to Worcester Street.

Gardiners'

Apart from John Moffatt's butcher's shop on the corner of Alvin Street and London Road, the first of Alvin Street's shops - if it was a shop - was Gardiners' Leather Supplies. I would come to know it well, for I was to be sent there often for my father's shoe-repairing supplies. My first call there is still engraved upon my memory.

"It's just past the off-licence, Donald, a scruffy place, set back." My father had said. "Looks empty and grubby and forgotten. Push the door hard. It won't be locked – it sticks."

As I approached the shop I saw that it was ancient and gnarled, a relic of the past with its worn bricks and dust-dulled windows. After a tussle with its warped and peeling door I lurched in, onto the bare wooden floor of a high-ceilinged and archaic den of dust and disorder and grime-sagged cobwebs, to be greeted by the smell of leather and ink and wax, the stuff of cobblers' shops that seasoned my young life.

To my left was a wide wooden counter that had once been proud but was now tired and worn under a century's jumble. I recall a tarnished oil lamp, an ornate letterpress, an ancient pewter-cast till (barnacled and carved), some tottering sides of leather, a few lost soles and heels, a mess of empty boxes, and a parade of forgotten cobbler-shop placards faded to blue. I walked to the counter and waited, but no one came, and as I lingered and hung about I idly glanced at them.

'Redferns for Rubber Heels' sighed one. 'Insist on Philips' Stick-On Soles' croaked a second, picturing the well-shod soles and heels of a hastily departing burglar. 'Leather for Health', gasped an unconvincing third, and a fourth depicted, as I recall, a spirited cane-wagging professor proclaiming: 'I am Master of my Feet and Captain of my Sole'.

There was a crop of modern placards, too, all properly stood up on a side-counter. I was to get to know them well, over the years, with their sober illustrations of well-bred and well-off goody-goody couples, each overtly celebrating their leather-bestowed health and happiness. The slim, Marcel-waved ladies with their leather handbags and their sensible, predominating shoes, smoking their Craven 'A's in long holders, and their slick and slim and bright-eyed blades with their pencil-moustaches and their stuck-down Brilliantined hair, roguishly inviting them into their little crimson open-topped sports cars...

But this day my musing came interrupted when a slight, hump-backed and stooped old man came scurrying from the shadows behind me, intent on walking past me towards the high glass-fronted box of an office, well behind and above the counter. He saw me, stopped, turned on his feet, prised his head towards me and twinkled his bright eyes, and as I looked at him I saw that he was of another world.

He was immaculately dressed in an old-fashioned frock coat, and the shiny high collar of his white pleated shirt was banded by a tie fashioned to a bundle of bows. His pince-nez glasses were secured to his waistcoat by a silk cord, and he peered over them as he spoke to me.

"Are-you-being-attended-to?" he asked, in a clipped and dry voice. His brisk and perky manner spoke his authority and breeding. Here was a spry, up-together and educated gentleman, I thought. Obviously Mr Gardiner.

"Not yet, sir." I said. He nodded me a smile, took his watch from his waistcoat pocket and blinked at it, and danced on to the office. And as he entered it, so a routed sketch tumbled out and ambled down to me in a low slouch. He was short, unbelievably scruffy, had rheumy eyes and a spreading, dew-dropped nose that had long abandoned its battle with the bottle.

He was obviously Mr Gardiner's 'boy'. He uttered no greeting, but took my list into his mittened and lumpy hands, stretched his arms, craned his head back and pulled his eyes to slits to read it, then he turned to his shelves and began tossing my assortment of leathers and rubbers and tingles and waxes onto the counter.

Then he took a stub of pencil from behind his ear, scanned the counter top for a clear spot, added some figures to the scrawls already there, sniffed his dewdrops out of sight and looked at me.

"Six an' fourpence 'a'penny." he growled, and snatching my ten shilling note into his grimy hands he threw it into the counter drawer, assembled my three and sevenpence ha'penny change, slapped it onto the counter nearer to himself than to me, and scuffed off out of sight, leaving me to gather up my change and my bits and carry them out as well as I could.

I had just had the pleasure of meeting Old Harry, who would treat me to the same sequence of events every time I called at Gardiners'. I never saw another customer there, never saw Old Harry smile, and never had the goods I bought put into a bag or a box.

Mrs Hamer's

Mrs Hamer's fish and chip shop, roughly opposite Gardiners, was the only one to I knew to offer savoury patties with her chips. Later she broadened her range to include raw carrots. It came about like this:

During the early days of the Second World War there suddenly came a noticeable increase in the number of enemy aeroplanes shot down over the south of England. This was, in fact, due to a new and highly secret British development known as Airborne Radar. The man entrusted with the trial of the prototype was one Group Captain John Cunningham, a highly distinguished and dedicated young test pilot. The unit was fitted into his Blenheim fighter 'plane, and his air-gunner, Jimmy Rawnsley, was swiftly retrained to operate it. And on the night of November 19th, 1940, the secret invention enabled Cunningham to shoot down three German 'planes.

His successes continued and 'Cat's Eyes' Cunningham, as he swiftly became known, became nationally recognised and applauded for his exceptional abilities. Meanwhile, the Ministry of Defence, anxious to suppress any inkling of the Radar invention from the Germans, ascribed Cunningham's success to his hearty but fictitious consumption of raw carrots which, they insisted, contained a substance that dramatically improved his ability to see in the dark. The story achieved further veracity when Lord Woolton, the new wartime Minister of Food, faced with the task of persuading British housewives to make more use of home-grown vegetables – including carrots – happily joined forces and exploited the story.

Whether this fooled the enemy I never knew, but it fooled the British all right, and to counteract the blackout we children were encouraged to eat raw carrots too. Even to take them to school for our lunch. The result was a national increase in the demand for carrots, and when Mrs Hamer bought in tubs of really large and tasty ones, her shop became our carrot centre. We bought them at a ha'penny each, devoured them greedily and (we convinced ourselves) shot eagle-eyed.

And in support of this, we'd cite the circumstances surrounding the advertising sign that was painted high on the right side of the Co-Ops' Alvin Street 'stores'. Britain feared a German invasion at the time, and so as to confuse any parachuted invaders as to their whereabouts, all place names on signs and fascias throughout the land had to be painted out. But the Co-Op missed the Clapham one, and the word GLOUCESTER remained boldly emblazoned across its width.

But nobody noticed it, until, a few days into our carrot-eating spell, we lads happened to look up and spot it. We jabbered our news to the first grown-up who chanced by, who happened to be the excitable and voluble Mrs Wilde. Immediately fired by the fear that the very heart of Clapham might become the centre of a German spy ring, she hastily and noisily gathered and convened an action group of lumpy and pinafore-clad patriots directly beneath it.

It didn't take them long to reach their conclusion. The country was in danger and something must be done, they thundered, and they marched in some sort of jumbled unison towards the Co-Ops' open door to protest.

There they met the luckless and loquacious George, of the fats counter, who was coming towards them armed with a long billhook. They stopped him in his tracks, eyed what they saw as an offensive weapon, pointed out that 'his' Co-Op was screaming Gloucester's whereabouts to the enemy, treated him to a rowdy lecture on Patriotism and the dire penalties for Aiding the Enemy, and all but accused him of being a Quisling. This was all too much for the simple George, who maintained that he had no idea what they were all on about and had only been coming out to pull down the blind. But as soon as he broke free he hastily set about broadcasting the news of his assailment to his Co-Op workmates...

It wasn't long before the management got their man around with a long ladder, a red face, and a pot of black paint. And he did a good, if belated job. At the time of writing, his handiwork can still be seen after more than sixty years, and I took a picture of it the other day. (Page 61)

Dorothy Davidson's

But the Clapham shop I remember best, the one that pushed the others from our minds each morning, was Davidsons'.

Dorothy Davidson's Alvin Street bakery was an oasis of morning magic to every schoolboy in Clapham and beyond.

Her wooden counter ran from the left of the front door, towards the back of the shop, and at its far end, just on the customers' side, a curtained archway ran to the bakery which lay behind.

Davidsons' were famed for their toffee-steeped dripping cakes and their currant-crowded Chelsea buns, but it was their hot and soft flour-dusted batch-cakes that drew us in the morning. Pulled and gathered from afar by its reputation and its baking-bread scents, we'd converge there in our throngs on our way to school to find her arid shop crammed to the door with a babbling mass of expectantly waiting schoolboys, and, behind the counter, a listless, face-fingering Dorothy still suffering from her last melee and nervously fearing the next, for her shop exploded afresh as each tray sailed up from the bakery.

It was an invigorating start to our day. We'd press ourselves through her door and into the crowd and jostle towards her counter whilst reading the signals of those closest to the curtain. It was they who'd detect the dull thud of the bakery door and first hear the ancient and dusty baker's plodding footsteps advancing up the passage, and when they did we'd see them straining forward, with one hand clutching the ha'penny that would be Dorothy's and the other formed into a grab for the nearest - and biggest – batch-cake.

So we'd wait there expectantly, hanging in limbo as the seconds tapped by, waiting, waiting, for the tell-tale signs...

Then it would happen! Those nearest the passage would come stirred and tense, and the shop would slip silent. We'd hear – or feel - the baker's pounding footsteps, and the tray of steaming goodies would shoot through the curtain in his cloth-clad hands.

And as the shop exploded into uproar Dorothy would fly galvanised and fidget to a dance and wag her finger at the bobbing and weaving sea of faces with a newly contrived and bravely marshalled show of authority.

"Now!" she'd cry, as though determined, for once, to sell her batch-cakes her way. "Now!" But her admonitions merely served to feed the growing pandemonium.

"Ooh! Smell them batch-cakes!!"

"That big 'un's mine!"

"It 'ain't, its mine…"

"Come on, come on, it's the cane if we'm late, mind!"

And there'd explode the abandoned free-for-all, the surging crush towards the tray, with shouted accusations of pushing and shoving and cries and yelps about clumsiness and trampled-on feet, as a sea of hands wove and flew and grabbed at the batch-cakes and stabbed and poked their ha'pennies at Dorothy's flailing hands, with the winners pushing to get out, the hopefuls shoving forward, and those at the door in jostled disarray.

And behind her counter, blinking like an owl and gaping like a fish, would be the thoroughly routed Dorothy, all ajerk, and dancing and twitching and gibbering, and waving her arms like some demented semaphore machine, desperately fighting to supervise her sales, collect her ha'pennies, and keep her reason.

Many's the time I saw the tray ravaged before it had left the hands of the luckless baker, and witnessed his hopeless face as he turned and tumbled it back through the archway to the refuge of the bakery.

It was a routine that was enacted several times every morning until the last tray had been cleared. Then, as the school bells called their stern message the shop would fall suddenly deserted, leaving Dorothy slumped against the counter with her eyes closed and her fingers to her head, wrung out for the day she'd scarcely begun...

One day, having left home too late for my morning treat, I called there on my way back from school to console myself with a cold Chester cake, only to find that the shop had grown another personality. It was silent and bare, strangely devoid of its baking-bread scents and its throngs of frantic and sweaty urchins, with not a batch-cake to be seen, and with a placid Dorothy, oblivious of my presence, plaintively airing her worries to a lone customer.

Gone was the pandemonium, the babble and the morning magic. It was a different shop, a dull and sober place, and I noticed for the first time the well-worn linoleum and the bare and dowdy walls with their lone poster of a malignant-looking Hitler and its stark message: 'He will give no warning. Always carry your gas mask'. It was a stilling experience. But by the next morning the shop had come itself again, as wild and as frantic as ever, with us – and Dorothy - in the thick of it.

Later on, our mother bought our occasional teatime cakes from Davidson's after she found (she swore) a toenail in one we'd bought from Hewishs', in London Road. I would be sent to collect them after school, and I soon became used to the quiet and empty afternoon atmosphere of the shop. Dorothy was a decent and sensitive worrier, and most of her grown-up customers were her confidants as well, and I'd often hear her recounting, to one or another, what she saw as the inconsiderate actions of a supplier, or the brusqueness of an official. She'd repeat their conversations verbatim, using her own agreeably reasonable attitude for her lines, and flying to a sharp and rebuking style for those of her oppressor.

"...So I said to him, you know, how you do... 'Well', I said, 'it all depends...' " (Dreamily and inoffensively delivered).

Then, adopting the brisk attitude and the aggressive stance of her quarry, and raising the volume of her voice:

".... 'All depends?' he barked. 'All depends?' Oh, he really snapped it out, he really did, you know, Rose... 'All depends on what? Eh? All depends on what...?' " (Spat out).

Was Dorothy sowing her hopeless protests against her ongoing unfulfilled life? Did she find her world a joyless place of subjection and arrow shafts, and construe them as coming from the few outsiders she encountered in her constrained and narrow life? Maybe. Some reckoned that she had been put behind her counter at an early age, to escape at the end of each long day to nothing more exciting than housework, servitude, and ancient, if kindly,

21

company. She lived a long, long life, Dorothy, but perhaps it wasn't the one she'd have chosen...

Mr Maisey's

Next to Dorothy's was a tall and tidy house whose front wore two or three enamelled signs. It belonged to the quietly avuncular and up-together Mr Maisey who sold Sunday papers at his door. He was a self-effacing man of some charisma, Mr Maisey, who, it seemed to me, wasn't inherently part of Clapham and didn't quite fit in. A small and diffident man whose brick-red complexion set off his dark, greying hair, he plods into my mind in his brown pinstriped suit, always with his eyebrows slightly raised and a somewhat quizzical and unassuming expression on his face. We never really assembled our childhood measures of Mr Maisey, for we never heard him speak.

Mr and Mrs Rogers

It was different with Mrs Rogers' general store. Her husband, a friendly and bluff milkman, clopped his milk around the streets by pony and trap, and ladled it to his customers' jugs from its open churns, whilst his wife, a short and round woman, served in the shop.

We harboured strange prejudices, we children. We didn't much like taking our ha'pennies to Mrs Rogers'. It wasn't so much the crop of beady little cysts that adorned her shiny face like a scattering of pinkish pearls; it was, I think, more the way she stopped and narrowed her tiny blue eyes as we entered, and (we thought) stared at us suspiciously and coldly and endlessly, as though we were heinous public enemies...

I daresay she had us rumbled...

Keelings'

Keelings' the newsagents, on the corner of Alvin Street and Sherbourne Street, was the last of that clutch of shops, and I remember it for three reasons. They were quiet, practical and kindly people, entirely without 'edge', I was addicted to their ha'penny tubes of sweet tobacco, and it was in our rented room over their shop that I came to Clapham and to the world.

Almost opposite Keelings' was a tiny shoe repairing shop that jutted out and narrowed the pavement. It was my uncle Harry's place until the mid-thirties when both he and Grampy Bullock contracted consumption and the family came struck down with tragedy. But that's part of another story, soon to be told, among others, in Hovels and Haydust.

The rest of Alvin Street's shops fell nearer its Worcester Street end, and some registered in me more than others. Mrs Davis seemed to sell mainly greengrocery and bottles of pop, but her shop boasted little stock and no magic, and to me she always seemed abstracted, as though her mind was elsewhere.

A farthing would buy us a few sweets in those days, and if we children were given a ha'penny, it was as much as we could hope for. But there were times, occasionally, when we did better. The Golden Anchor in Southgate Street specialised in little boys' suits, and to ensure a measure of repeat business they always placed, in the top pockets of their suits, a couple of brand new and shiny farthings, or perhaps a similarly shiny ha'penny. In my early Kingsholm schooldays my parents took me there for a suit, and when I came to wear it I found, in its top pocket, a large and gleaming penny.

I valued that penny, and kept it safely in my trousers pocket for days after I started school. The temptations to spend it came with every day, but, after running my thumbnail around the rolling expanse of its rim I invariably decided against them. Until the sad, sad day that I weakened...

It was a cold winter's day, and after morning school I saw, beside the few displayed trays of vegetables on Mrs Davis's blueslabbed front, a crate of delicious-looking penny bottles of red pop. I went in and asked for a bottle and she motioned me outside, took my penny, and served me from the crate.

"Drink it up whilst I wait for the bottle." she said, and stood tidying her trays of greens. I unscrewed the stopper and tipped the bottle to my mouth, but it yielded only a trickle of pop. The rest was a frozen pillar of ice trapped in the bottle. I looked up at her.

"I didn't get much pop, Mrs Davis." I said. "The bottle's full of ice!" She took the bottle and held it up to the light.

"Ooh, so it is!" she trilled, and she dropped it back into the crate, plodded back into her shop, tossed my penny into her drawer and closed the shop.

I don't think I ever entered Mrs Phelps' greengrocery shop opposite. I never found greengrocery very interesting, and anyway, it seemed a grown-ups' shop, always busy with local housewives. And to my young eyes the tubby Mrs Phelps always looked disconcerted, out of tune with her life.

The Weavers' were oil merchants who lived over their shop on the corner of Alvin Street and Columbia Street, with their live-in helpmate, Emma. They delivered their paraffin by horse and cart, and weren't all that well off, so, after their evening deliveries, they slipped along the riverside lanes to cut and collect armfuls of long grasses. These they placed on their shop roof to dry into hay, which they stored until winter to supplement their horse's feed.

Emblings'

The Emblings' were both a well-known Clapham family and prominent members of its business community, and Dave Embling's little Alvin Street sweet factory, opposite Weaver's, lay hidden behind its painted shop window. They produced a variety of boiled sweets there in the 'Thirties, including butter drops, acid drops, pear drops, cough drops, and their well-known 'Gloucester Humbugs', all of which they made by hand, using moulds. They were also well known for their gingerbread and lettered rock, each batch of which started off as a huge, flat white tablet with the lettering let-in in red. They then fashioned it into a squat and stocky pillar which they rolled and rolled on a long table until it was reduced to the required thickness.

Dave's brother Jim had a similar sweet shop and factory in nearby Worcester Street, and a stall in Eastgate Market, run by Mary Ford, who had left school at fourteen and was 'in service' with the Emblings. On Saturday nights, though, Jim would show up at his market stall to employ the well-known Embling 'foghorn' spiel to sell his Bumper Bargain Family Bags of sweets. His antics always grew a crowd.

"Step forward, ladies and gentleman, and help yourselves to an Emblings Giant Bag of sweets" he'd bawl. "The bargain of a lifetime! And what do you get in the Emblings' Giant Bag? I'll tell you! You get a big, big assortment of our celebrated home-made sweets, a jumbo bar of chocolate, and even a sugar mouse for the baby! And what'll it cost you? Well, you'll never believe it! Not ten shillings! Not five shillings! nor three; not even two! Tonight, all I'm asking for this Bumper Bargain Family Bag of sweets and chocolate is a single shilling! A bob!"

"Look, somebody there has fallen over with shock! Be quick now, the rest of you, before I realise I'm giving 'em away and get sensible!" And the crowd, captivated by his infectious petitions, would surge forward and buy the lot.

When Jim died, he left the stall to Mary.

Apart from their business interests, the Emblings' were known and respected for their untiring charity work, and for furnishing the Clapham childrens' occasional street parties with their gingerbread.

A few yards away from Embling's, on the corner of 'Fish Alley', the local colloquialism for Clarence Row, the resolute Cissie Cromwell, in her long white gown, dispensed her chunky brown chips with astringent and kindly authority whilst her silent husband, his back rounded and his pale face glistening, stirred at the fryer and satisfied its fiery bowels with shovelfuls of coal. They worked long and hard, the Cromwells, and won their two sons a bluecoat Rich's education. They were a chubby and respectful pair, their boys, who were known to the local lads as 'Fish' and 'Chip' respectively.

Fish and chips came served in newspaper sheets in those days, and when the war came and the newspapers shrunk to a single fold, Mrs Cromwell insisted that her customers take their own. Nobody argued.

Chapter 3

Bet's Wonder Stores

On the other corner of Fish Alley was Bet's Wonder Stores, or Redburns', for short.

Redburns' full-to-the-brim sweetshop cum general store, Clapham's busiest and most colourful shop, came into the hands of Betty Redburn at five o'clock on the evening of 11th April, 1938. She was just fourteen, but selling wasn't new to her...

Her parents, Alec and Florrie, already ran a general store in Clapham's Columbia Street, which they'd opened in 1930, and Betty recalled being sat on a crate, outside the shop, at two years old, selling oranges.

She must have done well, for with her imminent release from school on the last day of term, 11th April, 1938, her parents rented a former cake shop in Alvin Street from its owner, John Newth, the well-known Gloucester caterer. Betty recalled it to me from her seventy-seventh year, just before her untimely death...

"Our mother met me from school on my last day and told me I was going to run their second shop." she said. "I was besotted with clothes and fashions, and wanted to spend my time working in a dress-shop, so I made a fuss about it, but in those days the young did as they were told."

"She took me to the shop. It was empty and John Newth was standing on a table, painting the ceiling. When he'd finished, our people stocked it up from a handcart they had outside and planted me behind the counter. The fascia read 'Bet's Wonder Stores'. I was the Bet, our mother was the Wonder, and our father was the Stores."

"When we were ready to open our mother looked at her watch. It was five o'clock. 'You've got until ten o'clock tonight to take twelve and sixpence - the first week's rent.' she said. Then they both went home and left me to it."

"But when I closed at ten I'd only taken twelve and fourpence. 'Well' said our mother, 'you've got tuppence to take first thing tomorrow to make it up.' "

The shop did so well under young Betty's management that they bought it twelve months later, and by the time she was twenty-five, her dream of working in fashions came true. She opened her own haberdashery and wool shop in nearby Worcester Street, which she successfully ran for over fifty years.

Meanwhile, Betty's mother, Florrie, took to the running of the store. A solid and kindly woman with a golden core, she presided there with a no-nonsense practicality. Intelligent, worldly wise and of Romany stamp, she was perceptive and quietly spoken and, like her daughter, had a well-ordered mind. And unlike most grown-ups of that time, she never talked down to us children. We liked her and referred to her as Florrie - but not to her face.

Redburns' Shop

It was a piled-up den of spilt-over treasure, Redburns'; a crowded cove of rolling adventure that offered everything and anything from groceries and greens and firewood bundles to hair slides, sweets and collar studs, and but for a clearing where she stood, her counter lay jumbled with its wares. And buried amongst them, somewhere, under a block of ham or a card of pencils or cuff-links, was her thick maroon credit book with its stub of indelible pencil. Most of her regulars bought their groceries 'on the book', and by the end of the day no Clapham shopkeeper could boast as purple a tongue as Florrie's.

Us and Our Ha'pennies

We often ran our ha'pennies to Florrie's. She'd direct her big brown eyes at ours as we entered, and give us her full low-key attention before dropping her elbow onto her counter and lowering her unfurling palm to the level of the coin in our hand.

"What are you goin' to have, love?" she'd ask, in her quiet and slightly husky voice, and we'd stumble out our needs, which often came with a sweet or two extra for luck.

Sometimes, though, when we were overwhelmed by the variety of her wares, and unsure of what to choose, she'd sum up our faces and patiently offer suggestions.

"A sherbet dab, dear? Some caramels? What about four of them marbles? Or a marshmallow? Go on, have a marshmallow, and have these couple of caramels with it..."

The gift often did the trick, but if we still dithered she'd look about her shop and try again.

"There's lucky bags, dear. Have a lucky bag, eh?"

Sometimes we did, and out we'd tumble clutching a blown-up lucky-bag with our surprises rattling in the bottom. They seldom set our hearts a-racing, though. A tin whistle, perhaps, with a caramel and a couple of boiled sweets, or a flick book with some aniseed balls and a raspberry chew...

Her Pop Machine

Then one day, when Florrie's sherbet dabs and marshmallows seemed to have lost their magic for me and my responses slipped low. She cocked her head, fixed me with her steady brown eyes, and tacked an extra goodie onto the list I knew so well.

"Why not have a nice glass of home-made pop, love?" she said, in barely more than a husky whisper.

I followed her eyes to a sparkling new machine on a stand behind me. It was a contraption like a sealed goldfish bowl over a wondrous array of tubes and taps and levers.

"It's our new Vantas pop machine," she said to a woman in curlers who'd popped in behind me. Then she turned back towards me.

"So it's a nice glass of pop, is it, Duck?" she asked.

I was to learn that the Vantas made its pop by pressure-gassing water and releasing it into a glass containing a raspberry-flavoured tablet. These came in mauve slabs stamped into little tear-off squares. It was the first pop machine I'd ever seen, and I think I may have been its first customer.

"Yes please." I said, as old Bess Yeates trundled in behind the woman in curlers.

"Now where did I put that slab o' tablets?" Florrie asked herself as she dabbed her hands among the sprouts and lollypops and cakes and fireworks on her crowded counter. Then Rosie Gardner ambled in, followed by old Arthur Manners, and she intensified her efforts.

"Ah, here it is." she cried, just as her potato man rolled up.
And to those collecting in her fast filling shop: "I won't keep you a minute, dears. I'm just a-makin' this chap a glass of pop." And in her haste she tore not one tablet off the slab, but a giant cake of them, dropped them all into the communal glass, shoved it under the globe's spout, and yanked down its lever.

The globe's water flew to a startling fit of swirling and hissing and squelching chaos, and a cluster of enormous bubbles chased and spun and gulped and winked in a crazy dance. Then she touched another lever, and it belched and hissed its charge to the glass.

Then she pushed the seething brew to me, and I knew that with all that went into its making, that pop had to be something special. I brought the glass to my lips and with its raspberry spray peppering my face, I took a mouthful...

Oh, special it was, that pop, special it was...

All too soon it was gone, and I was left with a saturated set of taste buds, an ozone-tingling tongue, a nose that wanted to sneeze but couldn't, and a pair of watering eyes. It had been a concentrated adventure, that Redburns' glass of pop, and its making had been a spectacle of wonder. Just watching the Vantas work was worth the ha'penny, with the thrill of the pop a priceless bonus.

Florrie's Social Centre

To the women of Clapham, Redburns' was much more than a shop. It was their communal meeting place, a sort of casual social centre that had evolved, over the years, into their refuge, their comforting hub of compassion where they might air their news and joys and woes.

It would slip to its busiest, spontaneously yet predictably, around mid-morning every day, and to drop in then was to find perhaps half a dozen women, sometimes more, and some of them in their curlers, nursing their purchases and trading their concerns. They knew no pretensions, only that the problems that flowed among them would be heard with involved understanding and practical advice and help. Then they'd discuss the trials of kindred souls not presently among them. And because their species bred realism they easily slipped to compassion when the need arose. As happened when Mrs Green mentioned Eileen Walker to Sis Larcombe.

"'Ere, Sis, 'ave you seen the state o' poor Eileen lately? Oh, 'er's gone that thin, an' that cough..."

"I know, Joan. I sin 'er yest'y. 'Er looked awful, and 'er's gone so pale. An' 'er no age with them four kids. 'Course, 'er never got over losing 'er twins out at Over. 'Er've 'ad 'er troubles, mind..."

"'Er 'ave; tha's a fact...." Then, quietly:

"You knows what I'm a-thinkin', don't y'u, Joan?" Her falling voice slipped to a whisper, and her lips shaped the words that were too dreadful to voice.

"'Er's in a Decline, Joan. I'm sure on it."

"Consumption?" And there followed the grim, silent stare, the gnawing of lips and the sad, slow nod.

"I'm a-poppin' in with a bit o' stew, dinnertime. I'm a-goin' to cook a bit too much, you know..."

"I took 'er a bit o' cheese yest'y, and a bit o' corned beef. Mary's 'elpin' her with 'er tidyin' an' Doris is doin' 'er bit o' washin'. It's what'll 'appen to 'er kids as worries me..."

And it was a sort of collective almoners, too, Redburns'. Those not school-trained might bring an official-looking letter to be read, and if its news brought problems, customers privy by their presence would inject their words of comfort or advice and the matter would become the centre of discussion.

"Rose, d'y'u think this might be from th' Infirmary? Oney we 'a'n't 'eard about ar babby's adenoids, not yet..."

There'd come a smile or two, an outstretched hand, and the letter would be unfolded and read.

"It's th' Infirmary alright, Bess. Adenoids 'n tonsils, they says. Want's 'im ther' Tuesday week."

"'Ow old is 'e, Bess?"

"Oney five. D'y'u think it's safe?"

"'Course il is, love. Look at our Brian. Always 'ad coughs 'n' colds 'til we 'ad 'is done. 'E was five, too, same as your'n, and we 'a'nt never looked back. Don't you worry, Bess. 'E'll be all the beller for it..."

"Yeah, I 'ould too, Bess. 'Onest I 'ould. Don't let old Gibbie put y'u off. 'E's as ig'rant as a pig, an' a bit rough, an' he makes the little nurses cry, but 'e doos a good job." (Mr Van der Wet Gibb, a South African, was an extremely ignorant, uncouth and ungracious Royal Infirmary ENT consultant).

"Oh well, per'aps I'd beller. 'Ow do we fill this form in, Rose?" And as the reassured soul left with her problem committee-solved, they'd voice their sympathy for her trials.

"Poor devil. 'En't 'er rough-gellin'? 'Er don' 'ardly look up to it all, do 'er..."

"'Ere, 'eard about Vera James, Vi? 'Er's 'like that' again. 'Ad to go to the doctor's las' Tuesday and kept 'er Maisie off-a school to look after the babby... An' didn't that Boardman get round ther' fast an' collar 'er. Oh-ah, reported 'er, 'e did. Now, where's 'er goin' to get the money from, to pay the fine?"

"S'a cryin' shame, Chris... Wish I'd a'known, I'd'v' 'ad the babby for 'er. I will, nex' time..."

Alec's Shop

Alec Redburn, who ran Redburn's Columbia Street shop, was a lean and energetic worker with a crop of curly ginger hair. He was both a practical realist and a considerate and caring soul, the sort of man who would spontaneously help anyone. He was less philosophical than Florrie, though, and could be fiery if consistently provoked. During the war when everything was in short supply most shopkeepers were loyal to their regular customers, and any little luxuries were kept 'under the counter' until they came in. But some of the streetwise used to 'do the rounds' of the shops to get more than the rest.

One day I called at Alec's to find a coven of four or five gipsy women badgering him for the luxuries they were convinced he was hiding. They'd obviously been at it for a while, for there were half a dozen of his regulars waiting behind them.

"What's in that box on that shelf, mister?" asked one of the gipsies.

"It's empty." said Alec.

"Ah, but what's in it?" she insisted.

"It's *empty*." he said.

"Open it, then." she said. "I wants to see fer meself." Shaking his head and blowing through his teeth, Alec stretched up for the box and opened it. It was empty.

"What's in that tin down there?" she asked, and again he had to open it before she accepted that it was empty.

"What's under the counter, then?" countered the woman.

"There's nothing under the counter." he said.

"Let me see." she said. He looked at her, then motioned her round to look. There was nothing there, and I could see that Alec was beginning to simmer.

"What's in that drawer?" asked the woman. Alec studied her again, then beckoned her forward as though to reveal some good news, and shooting her eyes at her companions she leaned forward to hear him the better. His whispered message was over in two seconds, at which the woman pulled her face to a malignant expression, straightened, and strode out and up the street, followed by her puzzled but compliant associates.

I often wonder what he said.

Alas, the likes of the Redburns' are gone beyond recall. They were a decent, earthy clan who'd come up the hard way and I never heard a word against them. Alec's maxim was to treat people properly and to sell them what they wanted as long as it was inoffensive. In those days snuff-taking was a common and widespread comfort in Clapham, and Alec sold the stuff cheaply and loosely - by the ounce!

Florrie, a Romany who had gathered and sold firewood around the streets in her childhood years, knew both human suffering and the value of money, and was a woman of great humanity. And she was, perhaps, one of the most accidentally recruited and unprofitable of pawnbrokers ever. Being Romany, her few items of jewellery were of heavy gold, handed down through the generations. Local folk on hard times who had similar items would bring them to sell to her, but when she knew that an item was of sentimental value, Florrie would keep it ready for redemption in a sweet jar under her counter. But often the money she advanced was akin to the value of the items left, and many never came for their redemption.

I recall walking into the Cross Keys Tavern in Cross Keys Lane early one summer evening during, I suppose, the 'Sixties, to see Florrie alone at the bar, buying herself a Guinness. She was now a regal and rather heavy lady, and as she put her change away the landlord made a good-natured joke about the size of her capacious handbag being in keeping with her wealth. She nodded briefly before answering, in the quiet and husky voice I knew so well:

"I be a bit better off than I was, Chris, it's true, but mind, we've worked hard for it all our lives. Damn' hard...."

The landlord, at once serious, nodded understandingly, and Florrie patted her handbag.

"When we started, I couldn't run to an 'andbag." she said. "Never had one. Any bit o' money we made we kept in a paper bag."

The Co-Op

Alvin Street's Co-Op, known to Clapham as 'The Stores' was a plain, sawdust-floored place of wide wooden counters, butter pats, cheese wires, staff who'd been there for ages, and non-stop homely banter. The shop radiated an air of relaxed congeniality, due in no small part to the cheerfully loquacious George of the fats counter, who could pare half a pound of butter off his block with one swipe and pat it to its oblong, Wheatsheaf patterned perfection in no time. George was never still. Nor did he ever stop talking, but to go there and find him missing was to enter a duller shop strangely devoid of its life. He was entirely without edge, too, and every evening, as closing time loomed, he'd chatter his way to the back of the shop, slip on his pair of gumboots, and water the sawdust floor with a giant watering can before sweeping it clean for the morning.

The Butchers' Shops

The butchers' shops had sawdusted floors as well, and their walls were often lined with entire carcases hung from hooks that wheeled along their supporting bars. Their slaughterhouses were usually an adjoining lean-to shed or open yard, and the butchers bought their animals from the market on Saturdays, drove them through the streets to their yards and remained closed on Mondays whilst they killed them. It was common for an animal to escape from a slaughterhouse, and we lads often pursued them, sometimes for a mile or two into the country, for what we saw, in our insensitive minds, as sport.

I don't recall any refrigerators. Instead the meat was kept packed in ice, which came from the ice-works in huge slabs.

Mr Moffatt's

Flies were everywhere. In summer John Moffatt, whose shop was on the corner of London Road and Alvin Street, kept a circular glass beer-charged flytrap in the centre of his window, and we often lingered there to watch its entrapped victims, roaming around its interior with nothing to do but drink themselves to their oblivion.

There wasn't much ceremony to life in those days. Mr Moffatt used to hang his sheep carcases by their back legs across his shop-front doorway and chop them down the middle, and his customers had to stay his elbow and duck and skirmish under them to get into his shop.

Mr Townsend's

Mr Townsend the pork butcher cooked his chitterlings on Fridays, and sold them steaming hot to those who took their dishes. And before closing on Saturday nights he sold off all of his stock, starting with the meat and progressing with the sausages and faggots, and, last of all, his tasty home-made brawn. This usually sold at sixpence a pound, which was good value to start with, and he didn't like selling it for less.

The cannier women knew that the longer they waited, the cheaper the brawn would get. Late one Saturday night our mother joined them, and they all stood outside his window biding their time. Sixpence, read the price tag on the brawn, so no-one moved, and the butcher glanced their way and began tidying his shop.

The game had begun.

The moments passed, he carried on with his tidying, and the women stayed put. He changed the tag to fivepence. Nobody bought. He scrubbed at his block, looked about him, pulled a face or two, and changed the tag to fourpence. One older soul shuffled in and bagged her brawn and scurried away, but the rest stayed there with their chins up and their purses closed, eyeing the butcher as he eyed them back.

Then, whistling silently and tunelessly he began to sweep his floor. The women remained huddled and motionless, each switching her gaze between the price tag and his face. After a while he put down his brush, flicked his eyes at the women and changed the tag again. It was thre'pence now. One woman bought, but the core stayed put. Stalemate reigned.

Having finished the floor he began to count his takings, and only when he'd finished that did he look at his watch and change the tag for one marked tuppence. At that the women surged in, smiling and babbling him their greetings, and bought all of his brawn. At their price.

Mr Jephcott's

After learning his trade at Tom Mahoney's butcher's shop on the Knapp, Wally Morgan went to work at John Jephcott's in Alvin Street. It was Wally who first introduced me to the magic of ice when we lived over Mahoney's, after chopping a piece off a slab for me to play with.

He had a skittish sense of humour, Wally, and sometimes, when the girls were playing hopscotch in the middle of the road outside the Alvin Street shop, he'd run out, still attired from head to foot in his butcher's gown and trousers, and hop clumsily into their games. They always screamed and scattered to the edges, leaving him pouncing from square to square whilst chanting his advice as to how the game should be properly played, and passing grown-ups would look across and smile. He was ungainly alright, and intrusive, and he knew it, but it all added to the fun. After all, he was simply doing it for devilment.

Mr Bint's

It was unfortunate for Mr Bint the barber that his optical deficiency rhymed with his name, and that this day a heat wave had brought a rash of customers to his shop. It was a sweltering day, and a few wayward lads began to romp their high-spirits around his open door. He did his best to work through the disturbance but gradually his breathing grew deliberate and his snipping scissors flew to biting and snatching. Before long he had managed to snip a customer's ear, making him yell and squirm in his chair.

His temper snapped at this and he ran outside to deliver a spirited tirade to the boys. Their response was to sally around him, just out of range, pulling faces and crossing their eyes whilst mimicking his snipping. He made a run or two at them, but he wasn't quick enough, and he soon returned to his shop and his occupied chair.

A few minutes later when all was quiet, the boys silently appeared at his door with their cross-eyed faces grinning inanely.

"Mr Bint, don't you squint!" they sang in unison. "Aw, don't squint, Mr Bint!" The barber threw down his comb, ran through the door with his scissors spinning on his thumb, and rang out a few appropriate curses. The incident struck his customers as uproariously funny, and he returned to find them all roaring and wobbling on their chairs in uncontrolled mirth.

"Ah, I expect *they'm* still laughing, too." said Mr Bint, picking up his comb and resuming his work. "But if I catches hold of 'em they'll be laughing on the other side of their faces." Then, as he snipped on, his face softened to a rueful smile.

"Mind, I was a bit of a bugger m'self at their age." he confessed. "I remember the time..."

Tartaglia's

Though originally from Italy, the Tartaglias were of Clapham essence, and they had the hearts of all. A happy and pragmatic clan, they conjured up their ice-cream in the kitchen of their tall and happily shabby house, which adjoined the 'Rec' in Sweetbriar Street. Their serving freezer rested just inside their ever-open front door, and to hop onto their step with a ha'penny and swing the dangling bell was to pull one of them out, still chewing at their dinner, or carrying the paper they'd been reading, to cram as much ice-cream into one of their cones as they could, followed by a squirt of raspberry sauce. It was a struggle they always won, and we always came away from 'Tartags' feeling well done by.

A friendly and relaxed lot, they were generous and knew no affectations, and folks took them as they found them. When their son Tony was born, they gave free ice-cream to every child in Clapham.

According to the taste buds of Gloucester and those who struck national medals, 'Tartags' made the best ice-cream there ever was. It won prizes galore with predictable regularity, and Gloucester never knew its match.

Each evening Eric would stow a churn of ice-cream into his motorbike sidecar and clatter round Clapham and beyond, pummelling its klaxon horn as he circled to a stop. Out we'd run with our cups and glasses and coppers, to receive a dollop of nectar that sent us to heaven. Clapham without 'Tartags' in those far-misted days would have been unthinkable; like faggots without peas, or peaches without cream.

Chapter 4

Backstreet Dens

Front-room shops abounded in those backstreets. Tom Cambridge sold groceries and greens, and faggots and peas, as well as his thre'penny pigs' trotters and tuppenny hocks. And Mrs Stafford's ha'penny blocks of nutmegged rice peppered our tongues and melted in our mouths. Mrs Bick, her one-armed neighbour, sold firewood and 'penny briquettes' for the fire, which she made herself with coal-slack.

Because money was scarce, most of Clapham's little shops sold essentials and offered credit as a way of keeping a modest flow of income, and those of Mrs Huggins, Mrs Eley and Mrs Brinkworth were amongst them.

Front Door Traders

The depression of the early 'Thirties, with its widespread unemployment, created a level of poverty that is unimaginable to those who think themselves poor today, and one effect was that Clapham was a parish thick with its front door traders.

Mrs Poole's lemonade, 'made with real lemons, my dear,' was a ha'penny a glass, and when the weather was warm it came straight from of heaven. And Mrs Adlam's toffee-apples were the biggest and sweetest I ever knew. None came more golden or crunchy and juicy.

"Just an 'a'penny, luv, to you." she'd conspiratorially whisper as she held out her hand, and I felt privileged indeed as I parted with my coin - until I discovered that she said the same to everybody.

Then there was Mrs Pike's toffee. She made it, she claimed, from her great grandmother's secret recipe, and she could have been right. I never knew what was in it, and I don't suppose I ever shall now, but there was none like it. It was almost black, that toffee, as dark and deep and sweet as an opium den, and it glowed with its mystery. To put it to the lips was to court addiction, and it always won. Its tongue-melting magic was a tipsying brew that closed our eyes and slipped us to pastures of lawless wild honeys and caraway cultures of unashamed indulgence. To paradise, no less. A ha'penny-worth silenced us for ages. We shan't see its like again.

Johnny Green gathered and sold watercress, and Mrs Weaver made and sold her ha'penny squares of rice-cake. Mrs Bubb, who lived opposite 'Tartags' in Sweetbriar Street, made her bit of money from pigs' heads. She got them from the slaughter houses, cooked and sold the cheeks, and boiled the heads down to a tasty broth. And Mrs Etheridge, her next door neighbour, sold her home-made faggots and peas in gravy at fourpence a jugful. They were popular amongst Clapham's working women, particularly on a Friday, when they preferred to get off shopping with their bit of money rather than tie themselves to the cooking of their family's meals.

Like the rest, our mother would look out her biggest jug and send me to join the others at Mrs Etheridge's door. She'd fill the jug to the brim, and walking slowly and stiffly I'd tack myself along with the rest and negotiate my cargo homewards. They were delicious, those faggots and peas, and every few minutes one or another of the youngsters ahead of me would stop, take a look about them, and steal a slurp from their jug. And I was no better at all.

Services

Then there were those who offered services rather than goods. Mr Hayling swept chimneys, and Mrs Smart would get a girl out of trouble for ten shillings - less, or even nothing, if she felt she'd been hard done by. Then there were those like Mrs Yeates, who'd sit with the old and the sick, or run errands in the confident hope of a small reward. And there were those who were tied by their circumstances, or devoid of skill, and took in washing. There was no shame to it. Nobody looked down on them in Clapham. Times were hard; there was no Welfare State, and as the saying ran around the place – 'anything decent for a few coppers...'

Mrs Drinan, who lived in Columbia Street next to Arthur Mann's coal yard on the corner of Union Street, was the local pawnbroker's runner. Come Monday mornings she'd call on folks to collect their pawnings, and take them to the Pledge Office in St. John's Lane, for which she charged them tuppence. Pawning was a popular business among the women. They'd pawn their husband's suit on a Monday morning for five shillings, and redeem it in time for his Friday night trip to the pub for five and sixpence. Plus Mrs Drinan's tuppences, of course.

It was reckoned in Clapham that most of its men's suits covered more distance to and from Uncle's than they ever did on their owners. The men, of course, knew nothing about it, though it came a close thing when things went wrong, as they did for Lottie, Charlie Miles's missus.

Charlie was a keen darts player at The Magnet, and having reached the semi-finals of a brewery-organised match, his team was set to play against 'The Quart Pot', as The Deans Walk Inn was colloquially known.

Charlie's suit sailed off to the pawnshop on the Monday morning, and soon after a letter came for Charlie. When he got home from work that evening he opened it to learn that the match had been arranged for the next night, Tuesday, and a brewery big-wig would be on hand to present the cup. 'Sorry about the short notice.' said the letter - they'd had to shuffle a team or two about to fit it in. Charlie was as delighted as his wife was pole-axed.

It is a testimony to the good neighbourliness of Clapham's women that the moment Charlie left for work the next day they pulled together their rags for taking to Harry Stroud's yard, ran a few of their bits to Mrs Marshall's second-hand shop, and held a whip-round whilst Mrs Drinan stood by at the ready. As the day ran on they finally managed to collect the necessary five and six, and Mrs Drinan, waiving her commission, galloped off for the pawnshop. She managed to retrieve the suit as Uncle was about to close his doors, and Charlie, watched by many though their lace curtains, duly set off to help win the cup, oblivious of all the drama.

The Carrington-Windos were a popular and established clan. They came from Sweetbriar Street, where they lived, appropriately, in Carrington-Windos' Passage. Harry, the son, who had a butcher's stall in Eastgate Market, bought a hundred calves a week and slaughtered them at Ducks' Patch, a spot where the new Estcourt Road was later to cross the Kingsholm Road.

Harry's father, Danny, traded on a smaller scale. He would buy one or two calves and cook up their innards to make his 'Calves Haggis', which he sold for sixpence a pound.

Jim Clements

But for those whose trades were less essential, the depression brought severe poverty, even when they were highly skilled. Jim Clements of Swan Road was a self-employed master tailor of some note. He'd married twice and there were twelve children, and the family managed well enough until the depression struck and reduced his income to coppers. The trouble was that with money tight, folks could put off the buying of a suit. They made do with that they had.

As a self-employed man Jim couldn't claim dole money, so he took what work he could find, which was occasional alteration work. One customer was 'Professor' Deane, the eccentric who kept the neglected second-hand shop in Worcester Street, who got Jim to alter garments he had sold but which needed alteration.

Most of the scant work he got entailed the shortening or lengthening of trousers, for which he could command no more than thre'pence a pair, and this included the running about as well. The family existed in abject hand-to-mouth poverty.

When he'd altered a pair, he'd leave their ironing until the following morning so that when he lit the gas ring to heat his iron his children could take it in turns to warm their hands over the flames.

Having ironed them he'd get his son (also called Jim) to deliver them, and, if he was lucky enough to get paid on the spot, to buy a loaf of bread for the family's breakfast, from Melias's, where it was a ha'penny cheaper.

Jim's family was resourceful through necessity, as were most in Clapham. A Kingsholm cake shop near Sebert Street used to discard unsold fancy cakes that were past their best, and Jim's son would collect them to feed the family.

"They used to scrap custard-cream slices because the top layer of custard was 'going off,'" he recalled. "We used to get there before the dustmen, gather them and scrape the mould off, and have a feast of cakes we could never have managed to buy."

Johnny's jam and pickle factory in Skinner Street was a quality-conscious firm, and when they dumped their old wooden crates and empty jam-pulp tins into a small clay pit along Walham's 'Red Lane' at Sandhurst, they also dumped any fruit or vegetables that they considered stale.

"We knew all about it." Jim told me. "We'd collect them and take them home, and wash and eat them. Most of it was as good as anything in the shops. And whilst we were at it we'd take the wooden crates too, for our firewood. We *had* to do these things. It was the only way we could survive."

The Gurneys

Ron Gurney, of Worcester Street, (who, soon after he married was lumbered by his parasitic younger brother Ivor, the now celebrated poet) paralleled Jim's plight. He was a master tailor, too. When the depression came he had to close his Eastgate Street shop, and he and his seamstress wife Ethel had to scavenge for occasional work for coppers.

"Talk about desperation!" Ethel told me. "We got hardly any work and if it hadn't been for the toffs we'd have got none. Not that they paid much. I used to patch their worn-out clothes for a ha'penny a garment, and be glad to get it. And I don't know how many coats I 'turned' for 'em. To 'turn' a coat I would unpick all the stitching and turn the panels back to front so that their inside surfaces became the outside, then I re-made the coat so that it looked new. It was a lot of painstaking work for a very few coppers. I had to re-stitch the edges of dusters, too, and once I was given the job of making a blouse out of an old parasol. I spent days at it, but the panels were too small and tapered and I had to give up. Of course I got nothing for that."

All in all Mrs Gurney led a hard life, as my Aunt Nance was to relate to me in her autumn years.

Lanes' Farm

But folks found ways of stretching their bits of money to eke a living. Beyond the Christadelphian Hall at the back of Clapham was Lanes' farm, a place of vast acreage, where a cup of milk, straight from the cow could be got for a ha'penny. And on the way, there was always the chance of finding a few mushrooms, or even a few eggs, for roaming fowls were common then.

The Coalmen

When there was money, coal came next to food. Clapham had four family-owned coal yards, whose proprietors hauled their coal around the streets calling their presence and delivering their wares. Their carts were heavy when laden, and the enormous shire horses they kept to pull them were as much a part of Clapham life as their owners.

They were a polite and courteous breed, the black and glistening coalmen, typical of Clapham folk. They were strong and skilful, too. They marched their weighty and cumbersome cargos through our tiny rooms and kitchens without harming the furnishings or sprinkling their dusts, and when they reached the backyard coalhouse they'd flick their open-topped sacks over their shoulders with ease. Clapham housewives were a house-proud lot, but I never heard of one complaining.

45

The Coal Yards

Morgan's coal yard, in Sherbourne Street was owned and run by Walter, the father of Wally, the butcher's boy who worked at Mahoney's shop on the Knapp. And Mr Cratchley's yard, on the corner of Guinea Street and Sweetbriar Street served as his general stores as well.

Perhaps the best known of the coal yards' shires was Ben, Arthur Mann's horse, who, after each household delivery would walk unbidden to the next customer's house. Arthur's yard was on the corner of Columbia Street and Union Street, through a pair of tall wooden doors that opened onto the pavement. Sometimes we couldn't afford coal on the day he called, but if a bit of money came later, I'd be sent to his yard to collect enough for a fire or two. I recall the first time I was sent there with our old 'pram and sixpence ha'penny for a quarter hundredweight of coal. He had just un-harnessed Ben from his cart as I arrived, and whilst serving me he noticed that the horse was still standing still between the cart's shafts.

"Aw, go on in, Ben - I forgot." he called, and the horse instantly plodded over to its stable in the corner of the yard. I shot riveted as I watched it, straining my ears for its reply. I heard never a word, but I was forever ready to fetch the coal after that, and when I did, I always eyed that horse - and listened carefully - in case it had anything to say...

Alfred Orpin's yard was in nearby Suffolk Street. Short, fair and muscular, Alf was a natural gentleman, brisk, polite, and open, a man sprung for action before words. He humped his ebony diamonds to our coalhouse as though born to it, and when my mother pushed her coins to his short fingers I used to hover there just to hear him speak.

"Thank 'ee, ma'am." he'd wheeze as he bowed a bit and doffed his blackened cap. His voice, dragged from its carbon depths, was cracked and gravelled, a package of hoarse disharmony, and I relished its novelty. Once he'd re-settled his cap, Alf's slack-scuffing walk would roll him to his cart, where he'd toss the empty sack with the rest, climb aboard, and 'hey-hup' his horse, leaving his customers loving him - and clearing their throats.

He had a lorry, Alf, and a kind heart, and every summer he'd bring both to the fore and take Clapham's children to Bishops' Cleeve on their Sunday school outing.

Collecting Our Coal

It was a paradox that when we were snowed-up and needed coal most, it came harder to get, for the horses and carts couldn't get the coal from the wharves. I remember the first time I was sent to the railway sidings in Great Western Road to fetch some.

I wasn't very old. It was snowing a blizzard on top of thick and rutted frozen snow, and our mother wrapped me up, gave me a hot drink, pulled my jersey sleeves down over my hands, and sent me on my way. I pushed and juggled the old 'pram through the mounds of snow and over the frozen roadside ridges to the railway sidings along the line, and eventually arrived to find Alf dispensing his coal from a wagon.

Getting the 'pram there had been a trial, and it was worse bringing it back, laden with half a hundredweight of coal. It took me a couple of hours, and by the time I reached home again in the falling dusk I had forgotten the biting cold that had generated my journey, for I was hot and glowing, and moist with sweat.

Chapter 5

Earning a Crust

People didn't fly their disabilities in those days, they got on with earning their livings. Tripey Webb, who lived just inside Union Street, was an industrious soul, and quite a character in his polished gaiters. Although deaf and dumb, he managed to earn a living out of tripe. He regularly bought large quantities straight from the slaughterhouses, washed and bleached it, and sold it on to the local butchers.

Then there were the street traders. Fishy Stollard, who had a palsied arm, made his living by selling fish from his horse and cart - when he wasn't at the cattle market, collaring casual droving work.

Vera Stock, the Bread Woman, was a respected and grey haired soul whose barrow was really an attractively shaped cabinet on a pair of high wheels. It had a lift-up top, and when laden with loaves of bread it was heavy. She drew it by its shafts like a tired old thoroughbred, and seemed to count the cobbles as she walked. A gentle woman lumped by graft, she had a private, noble face, and a calm and measured manner, and she often wore a garlanded straw hat. She was troubled by an enormous goitre, and even as a child, her languor signalled me.

She was frugal and encapsulating with words, Mrs Stock, and those who heard her for the first time were taken with her brisk and cultured speech. But the truth was, she'd packed more into her life than hawking bread. She'd been, in her past, a governess to a large and cultured family.

These were times of easy perishment, and we never knew refrigerators. Like the rest we bought our bits of food fresh each day, boiled our milk in summer and salted foods down when they came cheap and abundant. One of the Bowl's street traders was the Salt Woman, whose cart was an old 'pram. It carried her mineral in great solid blocks, and she spent her days selling it round the doors.

"Salt..." she'd call in her soft low voice. "I got rock salt... Time to salt y'ur belly pork down... And them runner beans as is tuppence a pound... An' I got the salt... I got the salt...."

She kept a long thin knife atop of her blocks, and could slice off half-a-pound dead with it. I never saw a set of scales, nor heard her judgement tried.

There was the Fish Woman, too, who also pushed her wares around in a 'pram. A lost and mournful soul, she publicised her wares in the weariest of calls, as though her journeying had all but used her up and the holding together of her body and mind was as much as she could manage.

"Fish." she'd wail. "Fresh fish, 'ere at y'ur door..."

She advertised no conviction, but Clapham bought her fish because it kept her life. She was part of Clapham, and, they reasoned, part of them...

A far more cheerful contributor to Clapham life was Mrs Royles, of the industrious Walham family, who regularly came round the doors pushing her laden 'pram. She sold flowers at thre'pence a bunch and pegs at tuppence a dozen, and when we went fishing of an evening we'd see her family bunching the flowers and making the pegs around their wood fire near their caravan. They crafted the pegs from osier branches, which they'd cut into sections, split and shape them, then bind the tops with a single loop cut from a strip of tin.

Theirs was a truly local industry. They gathered the osiers from the Walham riverside and pits, and cut the tin strips from the jam-pulp tins dumped by the Johnny Stephens' factory into the Red Lane pit that was the local tip.

Red Lane was the local name for the narrow, unsurfaced track that ran from Sandhurst Lane to the Walham brickworks then on to The Jolly Waterman, the former riverside public house. It was so called because its surface came heavily coated, over the years; with the red brick dust distributed along its length by the carts that carried Walham's bricks. The brickworks were closed at the outbreak of the war in 1939, because it was feared that their glowing kilns would present a night-time navigation aid to enemy aircraft, and they weren't far from a secret wartime radio station at the nearby Wallsworth Hall mansion. They never re-opened.

The Rag and Bone Men

"Any Ol' Ragbone?" The uncouth cry was common round Clapham, and was the signal for the trading of unwanted clothes or scrap to the ragmen. Not that much money would change hands. The ragmen themselves would be driven to their tasks by their poverty, and were in it to make money, not dispense it. Most of them soon learned to measure a householder's astuteness, and to shape their bargaining accordingly.

"'Ere, give us fourpence for these old coats, then. Come on, fourpence"

"Ha! Don't make me laugh, guv'nor! Can't do that! I won't never get tuppence-ha'penny from the yard! But – tell y'u what, though. I'll go to thre'pence-'a'penny if you'll throw in that old bike as well. An' that's more'n I oughta! Come on, now. Is it a bargain?"

But the wilier collectors from outside the Bowl knew how to fill their carts in areas rich with children. They'd buy a box or two of day-old-chicks from Hooper's stall in Eastgate Market, which was not far from Mr Strange's Cockle Stall, and offer one for each bag of rags. And as they travelled the streets their success could be read from the pavement pockets of youngsters over-tending their chicks, and endlessly feeding them their saucers of fatal bread and milk.

Once their rounds were done the ragmen would usually slip alongside the deserted railway arches that connected London Road to Worcester Street, to sort out their tottings. Any of the clothes that were wearable would be set aside to go to the second-hand shops, then the woollens and cottons would be separated for sale to the yards, usually Harry Stroud's, though Raggy Small of Tredworth was reckoned by some to be a bit more generous at times. Then they'd scrutinise the bottles. The returnable ones they'd take back to the pubs or shops to redeem their deposits; those that could be matched with stoppers would be sold to those who dealt in home-made pop, and the rest would join the rags to go to the yards, along with the old iron and the bones.

Eliza Zampetti & Fazzi Toscano

Buskers sprouted everywhere those days, though I doubt if any answered to the term. One odd pair cheered the locality in summer, both with their novelty and their barrel organ. He was gangling and chicken-necked, and she stood stocky and solid under a yellow duster hat, and they took their turns to wind out their music whilst sharing a white clay pipe fed with fag ends. He'd puff at it whilst she wound, then she'd puff whilst he wound. Their music was sweet and infectious to all but them, and the coppers romped in whilst they moaned their disenchantment. At one day's end they sat counting their takings on the pavement by the Coach and Horses.

"Gets wusser 'n' wusser." she groaned.

"'T'aint what it was, that's for sure" he confirmed.

She was Eliza Zampetti and he could possibly have been Fazzi Toscano. They were a meticulously clean couple of Italian extraction who lived in Sweetbriar Street, opposite Tartaglias, between Mrs Etheridge, the faggots and peas woman, and Mrs Bubb, whose living came from pigs' heads.

They stowed their barrel-organ away after the winter and sold ice-cream separately in the summer, she from a cream barrow bearing her name and pitched just inside Alvin Street on its Worcester Street corner, and he from a travelling wagon bearing the name of Fazzi Toscano. But the true identity of Eliza's partner is open to doubt, for there was also a permanent Fazzi Toscano ice-cream stall in Eastgate Market, tucked between its pair of enormous front gates.

51

Anyhow, the couple was rumoured to have been secretly rich, and there were those who swore to having seen them cruising around the Bowl in a Rolls Royce.

Elvering

The approaching elver seasons always promoted a scurry of activity amongst Clapham's blades. They'd busy themselves along the banks of the river or the Nunnies, each looking for a long and straight willow branch about an inch and a half thick. And whilst they were at it, they'd cut themselves a bundle of osiers as well.

Then they'd set about making themselves an elver net. They'd turn the osiers into a boat-shaped structure about two feet long and eighteen inches wide, and make the branch its handle. The net's fabric would be a piece of cheese muslin from Heals, in Barton Street, who advertised it as elver net muslin.

Having made their nets, they'd pull their accessories together. A lantern, a bucket or two, a fair sized galvanised bath and a few pillowcases to contain the mountain of elvers they hoped to catch. Whilst many of them would get their bulky trappings to the river on their bikes, others would button-hole a fellow enthusiast with a car, if they could find one. Cars, of course, were luxuries indeed in those days, and the few I ever saw bedecked with elver nets were ancient bangers that clattered noisily up the road chuffing clouds of blue smoke.

The elvers would eventually come swimming upstream in their shoals, close to the banks, and in hopeful preparation the elver-men would choose their spots and light their fires, both to attract their quarries and to keep themselves warm.

So there they'd be, the elver-men, wrapped against the weather and ready and waiting to ply their nets from dusk to dawn in the hope of making their fortune. But when would the elvers be with them?

Nobody knew for sure. They'd certainly come with the spring tides of March and April of course, but some seasons they'd come as early as February, and in others they'd still be about in May.

Each season the question came resolved by the keener men, who went to the trouble of casting their nets early and often, so becoming scouts for the rest. More often than not the elver-men would come home weary and empty handed, time after time, or sometimes they'd net just about enough for a feed, but sooner or later one or more would strike a shoal. Then the word would fly around Clapham, and that night would see an exodus of heavily laden bikes and bangers clattering and spluttering towards the river.

But what part of the long and bending river? That was always the question, for whilst the season lasted a fresh shoal of elvers would come about every ten days, and swim upstream at a speed dependent on river conditions and the weather. Jim Whitfield, Charlie's son, told me that as a rough guide a shoal might travel from, say, the Jolly Waterman, Jim's riverside home, to the Tar Works in a day, but to complicate matters, part of each shoal would get swept back downstream by the flow, to start again. So elvering was a chancy business, and the elver-men could only guess, then fly off to their chosen spot, hoping they were right. But even the most experienced were often wrong. Sometimes they hadn't travelled upstream enough, other times they'd gone too far. And since mobile telephones were half a century into the future, they had no way of learning from their luckier peers – even if they'd been prepared to tell them!

The thought that others might be making huge catches whilst they couldn't find an elver came very galling to most, and the travelling was cumbersome, for very few spots along the river were in convenient reach of the roads, and even those that were presented quite an obstacle course for the fishermen and their vehicles and their cumbersome paraphernalia. It could all be a wearying and flattening business, and often a cold and pitch black one, too, and those who hit the jackpot were reckoned to deserve the money they made.

And there were, sooner or later, always the lucky ones, and those who dropped into a shoal could make very heavy catches. The late lamented Charlie Whitfield, who was widely regarded as the greatest local river authority of his day, sometimes caught fifteen or more pounds at a single dip of his net. The riverside term for a catch of twenty pounds was a score, and he'd caught twenty-five score in three hours. The shoals thinned out about four in the morning, or earlier if fog came, when they'd drop to the bottom like a stone.

Elvers were a popular delicacy in Gloucester, and particularly so in Clapham, and the elver-men easily sold all they caught. It was common to see them being offered live at their captors' front doors, from towel-topped pails on kitchen chairs. The going rate throughout my childhood was sixpence a pint, and they measured them with a pint pot borrowed from their local pub (in return for a feed of elvers, no doubt...).

Others put their buckets or tin baths onto barrows or old 'prams and pushed them round the streets in the middle of the road, and we'd hear them singing out their wares:

"Elvers alive-o, a tanner a pint... Come on; give y'ur old man a treat and liven him up! Fry 'im some of these with a bit o' bacon..."

Live elvers were transparent and cooked ones white. Our mother didn't like frying them alive, so she put them in salt water to kill them first. They were tasty alright, but the sight of their tiny, black-eyed corpses piled on the plate in their petrified turmoil always tinged me with a secret sadness, and Dylan Thomas's words would slip to mind: 'So many little lives...'

Sambo Lane

Some local characters, of course, made their money by peddling their charm and roguery. Sambo Lane was a charismatic street entertainer with both a barrel-organ and an attractive singing voice. He was also a shameless and unrepentant burglar, and prominently painted on the side of his music machine was the legend 'Sambo Lane, the singing convict'.

He lived along the Sandhurst Lane on the left, just past the fork, at Ablodes' Cottages, with his companion, a smart, attractive and volatile lady known locally as 'Dirty Gertie'. She had a temper, Gertie, and during their frequent end-of-day rows at the cottage, she would loudly rebuke him over his latest exploits and the way he'd handled them. The police got to know of it and took to crouching beneath their roadside window with their hands cupped round their ears, and as soon as they'd heard enough they'd bang their way in and charge him. And down he'd go again.

Lucky-Bag Williams

Lucky-Bag Williams was a respected and hard-working character who was noted for his incidental luck on the horses. He made his living, though, by buying fields of standing crops from farmers and rising at three or four in the morning to pick and gather them. Then he'd sell them, both in bulk to market gardeners such as Manley Wixey, and to the public, from his handcart.

Although barely five foot five, Lucky-Bag was an energetic and spontaneous man with a penchant for swift and direct action. He once caught the six foot two Tom Phelps filching a cabbage or two from his handcart and lost no time in attacking him. A terrible fight ensued.

"Lucky fought like a demon," said a bystander. "He got his cabbages back and sent old Tom packing."

Not long before Lucky died, he and Jim Clements met in the market, and they yarned about the lives they'd had.

"Would you live the same life again, Lucky?" asked Jim.

"Yes, Jim, I would." said Lucky, looking him in the eye. "All again, just the same. I wouldn't change a thing. Not a thing."

As Jim said: "How many would say that?"

The last I heard, Lucky's son Ted still had a stall in Eastgate Market.

Tom and Jack Phelps

Tom Phelps lived in Portland Street but was practically a part of Clapham. Its figure of fun, its constant loser. A scruffy, ramshackle sketch, Tom was a casual drover and vagabond who consumed vast quantities of rough cider - known locally as 'Stun 'Em' - and traded his life for an alcoholic haze.

He was tall for an itinerant, Tom. Six foot two. A blowsy, loose-limbed man, he always looked overdressed in his roomiest of clothes, and I never saw him without his loose, barely buttoned old herringbone overcoat. He had a florid, loose and cider-logged face, pulled to something resembling a contented leer by his chronic drinking, and he moved with a lurching and rolling gait.

He frequented the Cattle Market, being game for anything raffish that might pull in a few coppers, and he managed to make enough to hold himself together and to pull himself apart with his drink. But he enjoyed his span and was always nursing some enthusiasm. Regarded by most as an amusing nuisance, his exploits were considered tedious by the police, who, not over-busied by real crime in those days, regularly pulled him in to justify their existence. He usually got a week or so inside, and we'd read about his antics in our sober 'Citizen'.

I remember his tussle with the Corona Man in St. Aldate Street one busy market morning. The Corona Man had edged his little delivery wagon to the side of the road and was re-arranging his crates of wire-topped bottles as Tom tottered up, clutching a cider flagon. At the sight of the wagon of soft drinks Tom pulled his face into a leer of derisive laughter.

"'T'aint no good to man n'r beast, that stuff!" he blurted, waving his flagon in the air. "Now, if you was sittin' on a wagon full of these, you'd be a bit o' use!" And after hopefully tipping the empty flagon to his upturned lips he tossed it among the crates on the wagon.

"Drunk again, Tom Phelps, and the day barely started!" admonished the Corona Man as he removed the bottle from his crates. "You'll go to the devil for sure, Tom Phelps." But his admonitions fell on deaf ears. Tom belched, wished him all the best, and lurched on, his bleary blue eyes alive with the mischief he was yet to create.

Tom's brother Jack was far more up-together, and an even greater character. Six foot six tall and built to match, the straight-backed and swarthy Jack had a healthy brick-red complexion and a head of thick black hair, and was a familiar sight around the Bowl. A tough-looking but cordial man, he was flamboyantly quiet, had an astute business head and was a successful gambler who ran an illegal but busy Bookie's business in Black Dog Yard. He also reared pigs on a piece of land opposite Plock Court, and at any one time their numbers would range from fifty to a hundred.

Originally from Portland Street, a small cobbled road that then connected London Road, through Pickfords' Yard, to Henry Street, he often cruised around the Bowl in his immaculate and picturesque pony and trap, strikingly dressed in a black tuxedo, maroon waist-sash and a black ten-gallon hat, and smoking a giant cigar. At other times he was to be seen gently negotiating the crowded Northgate Street area in his enormous open-topped American car about the crowded city streets. A quietly friendly and contented man of dignity, he was a contrast to Tom alright, and a pointer, perhaps, to what Tom might have been had he not fallen to the drink...

'Professor' Deane

These were the days of eccentrics, and Clapham knew its share. One was 'Professor' Deane who kept a shop known as Deane's Wardrobe Dealers in Worcester Street. In its time it had been a high-class second-hand shop but by the 'Thirties it had fallen to neglect. Its large window lay bare and its few old-fashioned dummies reposed in the shadows in their various stages of undress.

The 'Professor' was a stout man who kept a monkey for company, and was known for studying the stars and for telling people their fortunes from the structure of their skulls. 'Professor Deane. Bumps Read' ran the sign on his door.

He was a keen angler, too. Every pub had an angling club then, and at competitions, before casting his line, the 'Professor' would dip his hand into his trousers pocket and throw a handful of coins into the river.

"Let's try bribing 'em to bite." he'd say. He was an amusing eccentric alright, but he had a hard core. One day his monkey made the mistake of nipping his hand and he promptly had it destroyed.

Mrs Sorrell

Mrs Sorrell, a woman whose life of grafting had left her heavy and lumpy at fifty, had come deranged when her husband left her for a younger woman. He constantly loomed in her every thought and she sang his praises to all.

"'E's good to me, my 'usband." she'd assert to passing strangers. "'E sends me postal orders from the kindness of his 'eart." And she'd wave an order, usually for one-and-six, the price of a pot of jam.

She kept a dozen big pennies in a jar on her shelf, and they remained sacrosanct, even when she was hard up for food.

"I'd never part with 'em." she'd say. "Not to pay bills nor nothin'. My 'usband gave 'em to me, to 'phone him when he gets a telephone. 'E'll be back, one day. 'E loves me from the kindness of his 'eart. 'E told me so 'isself. 'E'll come back alright, you don't wanna bother. I knows it..."

One day I saw him with his other woman. Mousey, dumpy and sluggish, she looked an unattractive and unclean mess. But then, so did he. They made a fatty, pallid and shallow pair, the architects of Mrs Sorrell's misery.

Betty Redburn and her mother Florrie at their home behind their
Columbia Street shop

Florrie Redburn outside her shop and, next door, Dave Embling's former
sweet factory

Photo: Donald Bullock

Aunt Nell, Syd Lander's long-suffering wife

Photo: Donald Bullock

'Archie Workman' and his goose*

Photo: Donald Bullock

That Co-Op sign, photographed recently

Photo: Donald Bullock

Pitch and Toss on the Rec*

Charlie Whitfield, who made the
original Jolly Waterman his family
home when it ceased trading as a
riverside pub in 1921

Photo: Jim Whitfield

An early studio photograph of Alec
and Florrie Redburn

Photo: Betty Dix

Jim Clements, photographed
in the garden of his
Sandhurst home

Photo: Molly Clements

Jenny, Albert Workman's wife at
their Columbia Street home

Photo: Betty Dix

Photo: Donald Bullock
Gossiping group outside Redburns'
(with Aunt Nance on the right)*

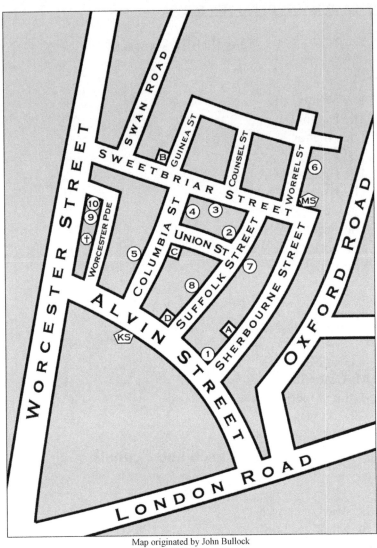

Map originated by John Bullock

Map of Clapham, with its many public houses, its coal-yards, church and schools, and, opposite, its key.

Key to map on previous page:

The Public Houses

The White Lion	1
The Magnet	2
The Anchor	3
The Pheasant	4
The Rose and Crown	5
The Duke of York	6
The Suffolk Inn	7
The Suffolk Arms	8
The Fortune of War	9
The Kingsholm	10

The Coal Yards

Walter Morgan's	A
Mr Cratchley's	B
Arthur Mann's	C
Alfred Orpin's	D

The Church and Schools

St. Mark's church	†
St. Mark's school	MS
Kingsholm school	KS

Photo: Donald Bullock

'Archie Workman' and his 'pram outside the Coach and Horses on
St. Catherine's Knapp*

Photo: L.E. 'Peter' Copeland

Fire training exercise in Alvin Street, with Redburn's shop on the right.
The shop opposite, with its blind down, is Mrs Phelps's greengrocery.

Letters

Free ices when Tony was born

MADAM – Reference "The Way we Were", Gloucester News, January 6, on local ice cream makers.

I was born in Foundry Row, number 11, and I well remember the ice cream lady, she lived in number 13 or 14. My mother always told me she was my Godmother!

She moved from there into Sweetbriar Street right opposite Tartags (Tartaglia's) as we always called them – even to this day – or her cart was parked there.

I clearly remember when Tony Tartag was born, there was free ice cream for all the kids around.

I will be writing a book if I go on.

An old Claphamite.
Mrs Gladys Oakey
(formerly Baylis).

Cutting: Gloucester News

Press cutting recalling free ice-cream from Tartaglia's

Photo: John Rowden

Centre of Alvin Street, looking towards Worcester Street, taken during Clapham's demolition. The pedestrian has just passed the little cobbler's shop which jutted into the pavement

Photo: John Rowden

Alvin Street from its London Road end. The white terrace building on the right is Dorothy Davidson's shop and bakery. The motorist is calling at Mr Maisey's. Two doors below is Mrs Hamer's shop, then Mrs Rogers's, and on the corner, Keeling's the newsagent. Gardiners' Leather Supplies is set back opposite Davidson's

Photo: John Rowden

The same scene looking towards London Road. In the foreground, left, is
Keeling's, then Mrs Rogers's, then Mrs Hamer's, and, in the background,
Dorothy Davidson's. Gardiners' is on the right.

Photo: John Rowden

View of lower Alvin Street looking towards Worcester Street. The grey-
fronted building before the corner is Weaver's Oil shop, and Mrs
Phelps's greengrocery shop is two doors nearer to the camera
Opposite (hidden) is Mrs Davis's shop, and below it, Mrs Cromwell's
fish and chip shop, Bet's Wonder Stores, and, next door, Emblings'
sweet factory

Photo: Betty Dix. Reconstructed by John Bullock

Bet's Wonder Stores, Alvin Street, on the right corner of 'Fish Alley'. On the other corner (not seen) is Cissie Cromwell's fish and chip shop. After 1925 'Fish Alley' led to Kingsholm School

Coronation festivities in Union Street, Clapham's heart, in the summer of 1953. Alec Redburn's Columbia Street shop can just be seen in the background, right. How flattening to reflect that even as this happy and patriotic scene was being recorded, plans were afoot to raze Clapham to the ground and to disperse its happy and contented culture to a mix of far away, alien and inaccessible plains.

Almost the end. Alec Redburn's shop, standing alone in its prairie of rubble, with its pavement display of vegetables and with Alec still in attendance, waiting for the customers who are gone for ever.

Chapter 6

Out and About

'Beardybum' Dunlop patrolled the streets of Clapham, and he was nothing if not a gentleman. In his immaculate swallowtail suit and spats, and with his top hat and silver-topped ebony cane he turned heads aplenty. He had a flowing, well-trimmed white beard and a thoughtful, inquisitive air, and whilst strolling he frequently stopped to carefully study passers-by.

But 'Catty' Kilminster's claim to fame was his affinity for felines. A seedy and abstracted man, he lived close to Aunt Nance in Worcester Street, and often went out walking with ten or more of his fat and pampered cats, all of them on leads and all straggling the wide pavement - except for the one he wore around his neck like a Nineteen-Twenties stole.

The fellow we knew as Montague added to the pavement cabaret, too. A tall, thin and springy cove with a thatch of languid hair and a moist and pallid face, and forever in a dirty trench coat, he paced about in long, leggy strides, with his elbows back and his chin forward, until some inner compulsion suddenly whacked him into a crouched, furtive and darting ten-yard run. Then, just as suddenly, he reverted to his former walk - until his demons triggered him again.

But those who laughed at Papa Jefferies didn't know him well enough. He wasn't as amusing as he seemed. He was the top dog at the Great Western Road workhouse, and he savoured his power. A small and tubby man of Pickwickian stamp, he dressed as behoved a Very Important Person, with his bespoke tailored suit, his gold watch and chain, his spats over his highly polished shoes, his black homburg hat and his ornate, tightly rolled umbrella.

He would come strutting along Worcester Street and Alvin Street with a haughty and self-important air, as though he owned everything he surveyed and was displeased at the prospect of his inferiors despoiling it. He claimed the centre of the pavement as his own, and when passers-by stepped hurriedly aside it was no more than he expected. Occasionally he'd stop and study a bit of debris on the pavement, a cigarette end or whatever, and switch his expression from one of disdain to one of pained disgust. Then he'd impatiently flick the offending item to the gutter with the tip of his umbrella, as though it was an insult to his vision. Clapham knew Papa Jefferies as an arrogant and pumped up prig, a man feared by those consigned to his workhouse.

The Nit Nurse

A common sight in those days was Miss Allen, the travelling School Nit Nurse who rode from school to school on a sit-up-and-beg bicycle whose back wheel was enclosed by skirt-guard stringing and whose handlebars supported a decorated wicker basket. She wore a full-brimmed hat, and because of her very short legs and high saddle her feet barely reached the pedals of her bike, so that she oscillated sideways as she went.

She called at each school once a month to check the pupils for infestations, but was never seen to touch one. She used a pencil to lift and part their hair and to move their cuffs and collars.

She called lice and fleas 'livestock', and when she found any on the child before her, she'd bawl out the details so that the whole class could hear, as she raised an appropriately coloured card.

"This one's got nits and lice. It'll be a pink card for you, m'dear. Tell your mother to comb your hair with vinegar and water, and I shall want to see you every time I call." Or:

"Aha! Fleas! Thought there would be! It's a mauve card for you, my lad – and I shall want to see *you* every time I call, too."

Once a card was raised it served as a lasting public label for the luckless child, to whom it was handed, in front of the class, before each of her subsequent visits...

Being caught harbouring 'livestock' was bad enough, but those with impetigo fared worse. She freely dabbed their faces with her bright violet antiseptic paint, and it wouldn't wash off. And it was worse still for those she found with ring-wormed scalps.

They'd be hauled off to the clinic in New Inn Lane where their heads would be shaved clean and freely purpled, so that they emerged, in the words of a Citizen contributor of many years ago, 'looking like Apache Indians'.

The Rechabites

Infections were rife then and medical attention was an important factor in our lives. Our family doctor was bound into the Rechabites movement and every Friday night I'd be sent to the Christadelphian Hall in Sherbourne Street to pay our dues.

I remember the first time I went there. It was a dingy and forbidding looking den from the outside, and as I pushed through its neglected doors into its little cream and brown painted hall, dust rose from its floorboards. It was gloomy, cold and bare, and lit by the dimmest of gaslights, and I could just make out a jumble of piled up chairs and debris in its shadows.

The collector, a tatty man in a bunched up overcoat and mittens, sat at a card table just inside the door. His trousers were wrapped round his legs and tucked into his socks, and his bike leaned against the wall behind him. His ledger and cashbox sat on the card table together with his Woodbines and matches and a stub of indelible pencil. He was a flabby-faced and rheumy-eyed man with a drinker's nose, and as I approached him he noisily sniffed its pearly pair of dewdrops out of sight.

I passed him our coppers and card, and as he rolled his woolly entries into his book and onto our card I fastened my eyes on his nose and watched his pearls rising and falling as he breathed. It wasn't a very jolly business, calling at that place, but the collector's antics added a little interest.

It was a teetotal benefit society, The Rechabites, founded in 1835 by a frenetic abstainer whose philosophy required those who joined to sign a pledge of lifelong abstinence. But fortunately for Clapham's men folk and its plethora of pubs - not to mention its dedicated but famously intemperate doctors - the founder's successors paid scant attention to the maintenance of their creed.

Deaths' Customs

The sadness of a local death was a happening shared by the whole street, and its community rallied in sympathetic and practical support of the bereaved. The first to be called was one of the local women who customarily laid out the dead. Perhaps Mrs Holland of Swan Road, or Granny Bullock, who always put on the white dress and apron and bonnet that she kept for the task.

Once that was in hand the neighbours would fall into a support group, with the welfare of any children uppermost in their minds. One or another would offer to look after them for the while. The death would be announced on a displayed blackboard and the house would be identified by the tacking of a strip of blackened wood vertically down the centre of its front window. Its curtains would be closed, as would those of its neighbours, and the undertakers would call to measure the body for its custom-made coffin, then put it in the front room, covered by a sheet, on boards supported by trestles.

Meanwhile two or three of the local women would raise a book and start a door to door collection, recording the donations towards a wreath whose card would read 'With love and respect from your neighbours'. Any surplus money would be handed to the bereaved. The family would then wear dark mourning clothes, and the closest neighbours black armbands, for weeks.

Syd Lander

Syd Lander, who lived in Union Street with his wife Nell, was a man without hope, and whilst he drew peoples' sympathy he courted no popularity. Tall and scruffy, loosely and lumpily built and morosely uncouth, Syd had suffered horribly disfiguring wounds in France in the First World War when a shell exploded in his face. They had pulled it roughly together, what was left of it, but its left side had been beyond their skills. The side of his mouth lay exposed, as did a gaping and bloodshot eyeball in its raw and watering socket, and Syd's hand was never without the red-spotted hanky he used for constantly brushing it dry.

His attempts at speech produced little more than hollow noises, and I shall never forget his hopeless appearance, nor his glaring look of resentful anger at the price he'd paid for the country that meted him his misery and poverty. Small wonder, then, that he lived for the drink that addled his brain, stoked his face to its angry fire, and drove him to his arrogant belligerence.

He made his living - if living it was - by pushing his shabby, canvas-covered barrel-organ from one cinema queue to another, and winding out his music to its seas of faces. When the queues were long he removed the organ's side panels to release more sound, and often, after two or three melodies, he'd ungraciously pull some luckless soul from the queue and gruffly set him winding.

"'Ere, stand like this, wind like that. Not too quick, not too slow. Keep it even." he'd command in his muffled voice, and having set his victim to work he'd barge along the queue glowering and pushing his greasy cap at every face.

If Syd hadn't been obtuse when the shell took his pride he'd learned to grow the condition since. He was a desperately unhappy man, a tortured soul driven to working the queues to buy the drink that rendered his life just bearable. By publicly winding his machine he was providing more than its addictive melodies for the coppers he received, he was dispensing his hideous appearance. And he knew it, but time had calloused his feelings and he no more heeded their scrutinies than he heard his sailing melodies.

I knew more of Syd than the rest of our group. That his wife Nell, a tiny, bent and suffering woman, fared badly at his hands, and skivvied for her housekeeping shillings 'til she died, for Syd's earnings and pension went on the drink that brought her his violence. Great Aunt Nell was my Granny Boden's sister, and Syd my great uncle.

But I never let on. Not to anybody. Ever.

The War

The 'Thirties was a decade of mass unemployment, poverty, endemic diseases and low life expectancy among the masses. The Establishment, to the working man, was all-powerful and unquestioned, and if its bureaucracy wasn't often over-used against the weak, it was there to keep them in check.

And yet there was an underlying happiness and contentment among the people, a patriotic pride and a code of common decency that must remain incomprehensible to those who never knew it. Although Great Britain was the hub of the world's greatest Empire, it was, to the man in the street, still an insular island with its own traditions and its own highly evolved way of life. National Pride rose proudly and unashamedly everywhere, Union flags rose in vast numbers at the slightest provocation, and the term 'jingoism' was an undiscovered word that society would have regarded as highly offensive if not treasonable. British was best, and no doubt about it. A single box of foreign matches spoke volumes for 'Sammy' Moreland[*]

Then, at eleven o'clock on a still and sunny Sunday, a bright, early September morning, just after the Walls' Stop Me and Buy One man had rolled up on his navy-blue box-tricycle and sold us our ha'penny triangular water ices, a sad and humble man's voice on our front-room wireless told us in his clipped and dry voice that from that moment we were at war with Germany...

My people fell as still as the air. The country we knew, that we had been born into and were growing up in, our way of life, the way we spoke, the very things we took for granted, all of these were set to disappear. Not just for the duration of the war, but forever...

It was the death of a unique and wondrous culture.

The air raids weren't long a-coming. Clapham heard the haunting wail of its first air raid siren early on the morning of

---

[*]Samuel Moreland, the founder of Moreland's Match Manufacturers in Gloucester's Bristol Road, who employed hundreds of young local girls who were widely referred to as 'Sammy Moreland's Angels'

Wednesday, June 26th 1940, and on Monday, October 7th, soon after dark, clutches of incendiary bombs fell on four Longlevens streets. And sixteen high explosive bombs fell at Matson on Thursday, November 14th, in the City's first daylight raid.

At seven in the morning on Thursday, January 2nd, 1941 two large bombs fell together, one on Napier Street and the other on Montpellier, killing sixteen people. And a fortnight later, on Thursday, January 16th, fifty incendiary bombs fell in and around Clapham, on Sebert Street, Sweetbriar Street, Suffolk Street, St. Mark's Street, Kingsholm Road, Denmark Road, Heathville Road, Sandhurst Road, and Edwy Parade. And St. Mark's Church suffered a direct hit.

My memory slips me back to four o'clock on the afternoon of Wednesday, March 26th, 1941. The Oakbank 'bus had just dropped us off from school outside Redburns' shop and as I arrived at our front door I heard the loud roar of a low-flying German 'plane. I looked up to see it ejecting a tumbling batch of tiny black canisters. They were its entire load of bombs, of course, for it was being pursued by a British fighter 'plane. As I rushed into the house to tell my mother we heard and felt the terrific crash of their impact followed by the crashing of glass. The crashing was the smashing into the road of the large plate glass window of a nearby shop. The bombs had fallen on Barton Street, Derby Road, Millbrook Street and the L.M.S. railway platform. Eighteen houses and a church were demolished, six people were killed, and twenty-seven injured. And so it went on...

Chapter 7

Archie Workman

Archie Workman was a man of contradictions, a mix of enigmas, a paradox...

A sketch of no account, yet a lobe of Clapham's heart. A work-shy bent on lifelong toil, and an unbelievably tidy scruff. He was shiftless yet reliable, a runabout going nowhere, and, as things turned out, both unique and of a pair.

The Workmans' lived with old Mr Griffiths in Columbia Street, next door to the Weavers, and were an aptly-named kinship of three; Bess Workman, a big woman, and her two sons Archie and Albert, both of whom were small and spare and of the same stamp, except that Archie, the eldest, was a shade taller. Otherwise, they looked alike, and as the wags of Clapham had it: 'You can't tell them apart unless they're together'.

The bit of pavement outside their house was often well endowed with the jumble of their living, and to step over it and through their ever-open door was to enter the active and unruly den of their money-making callings. I can still remember the time that Granny Bullock took me there to ask them to sweep her chimney.

Blackened bags of soot lay everywhere, and Bess was sitting on a pile of four, skinning a rabbit and quaffing at a mug of red wine. Behind her stood the old man, dusting and washing odd bottles and mating them with stoppers from an old cardboard box.

"Joo mind, ma'am?" said a quiet voice behind us, and we turned to see Albert at the door, leading a horse by its bit. We stepped aside and he led it through the house and out of the back door, then returned to the sorting of some rags across the room. Granny Bullock spoke to Bess about her smoking fireplace, and Bess called to Albert over her shoulder.

"Albert, ther's a chimbley come in, duck. Come an' see the lady, 'cos Archie ent back yet."

"'E's a comin', Mrs Er..." she said. And, as she tossed the skin aside: "Wanna rabbit, dear? Archie caught 'im 's'mornin' up the Nunnies. E's a good fat 'un, look. Worth a tanner, ent 'e? Give us fourpence, eh?"

As Granny Bullock eyed the sooty offering and quilped at the air, the spare and spry Archie stepped in from the pavement, looking for all the world like Albert, and carrying two buckets of milk on a yoke.

"Done well today, Ma," he said. "Got 'em both full, I 'ave. An' earned three bob. Joo know, I 'a'n't never sin so many milkers an' ther' calves ther'."

He'd been to the Cattle Market. On market days the latest crop of newly calved cows, with their udders distended and spraying milk everywhere, would be tethered to the pens near John Newth's coffee shack, just inside the gates closest to the Spread Eagle. And binder-twined to each, with its head pulled aloft, would be its muzzled and spindly calf. It was common to see urchins, itinerants and destitutes, the Workmans' often among them, milking the cows into old jars or bottles. Few bothered them; most reckoned they were doing the suffering cows a kindness.

Albert worked mainly at the house, whilst Archie was forever running about the streets with his piled-up 'pram, culling rags, moving rubbish, running errands and grubbing for remnants at sales. And on market days he'd skip to the cattle and fruit markets to get his milk and to turn his hand to any task that came.

And thus they made their livings, the Workmans', by selling their bottles of filched milk and what rabbits they caught, by sweeping chimneys, trading oddments gained by menial tasks, and by putting themselves to anything that came along. And as they worked at home they drew their contentment from the tippling of their home-made wine, which they brewed and drank in vast amounts from cracked and jaded mugs. They were a Clapham institution, the Workmans.

Then, as time ran on the old folks died, and so did Archie, well before his time. And Albert, thrice bereaved and alone, and needing to make a living, took up Archie's 'pram, answered to his name, slid about the streets in his place, and fitted to the jobs that came along. And those about the streets saw little change, just the image of the scamp they knew as Archie, a man built for action, short and slight and dapper, and perennially on the trot, running his old 'pram about the streets as ever. As scruffy as a vagrant, and never without his growth of gingery stubble with its Woodbine-sized hole in the centre of his lips, he was obliging, unassuming and quiet-voiced.

And so he carried on, in the only way he knew, living alone and working hard and long for the coppers that sustained him. And then he met Jennie, another lonely soul, who saw not just Archie the sketch, but his simple qualities, too. She pursued and married him, fed and looked after him, turned his unkempt home into a little palace, and brought him his happiness.

But it was not to last. All too soon she too died, and Archie, alone again, silently ran his grief about the streets whilst earning his living with his 'pram.

His Jobs

Where there was rubbish to be moved, he'd divine the fact and dance towards the scene to the melodies of his squeaking 'pram.

"I'll take it all away and sweep the place clean for a tanner." he'd say, or "I'll clear the garden, Ma'am, and dig it all for a bob." And he was as always as good as his word. He'd fling off his coat and throw himself to the task with bright-eyed zeal, and he wouldn't stop until it was done. And he was fair and honest, too, as the up-together Aunt Nance testified. She'd had him round to clear up after she'd had her roof repaired.

"How much to take this rubbish away and leave it all tidy then, Archie." she asked.

"'Ang on, Nancie, this 'en't all rubbish, y'know." he said. "Ther's some nice bits of old lead ther' as'll sell at Harry Stroud's scrapyard."

"Then it's all yours, Archie," said Aunt Nance. "As long as you clear the lot away."

"Nancie, you'm good to me," he said. "I don't want nothin' to take it all. I'll do it for nothin'. An' I'll sweep all the yard up, garden path an' all."

Well-liked in Clapham

Clapham knew Archie as a decent scamp of energy and enterprise; a non-conformist alright, but an industrious soul rich in principle whose feet were on the ground and who expected to work hard for the coppers that sustained him. And although his horizons grew close, he was, in his small way, the essence of a good businessman. He was honest, efficient, reasonable, polite, willing, available when needed, and reliable.

And this, together with his zest for life, won the hearts of Clapham's folk. They found his company warming, and liked him well, and many a cup of tea came passed his way through their front windows, often with a biscuit or two and a bit of cake as well. Archie warmed to the life. Not for him, the comfort or sanctity of a proper job. He preferred the spice of living as he pleased and was content with the coppers it brought.

The Goose

I remember one occasion, though, when he was paid in kind. And well paid, too, but it brought him problems...

I had done our mother's shopping at the Co-Op store in Alvin Street, and emerged to a terrible din of squawking and shouting accompanying a scuffle on the opposite pavement. Archie had been paid with an enormous goose for helping at the market, and the pair were locked in argument and combat. Astonished and intrigued, I put down our mother's bag of groceries and watched.

The bird, clutched in Archie's uncertain grasp, was proving a poor traveller, and with one wing free and flapping wildly it was spinning him about the pavement in cavorting circles. Passers-by stopped to rub their eyes and plug their ears and people came tumbling from their doors, among them the entire Co-Op staff in their long white gowns.

Then the goose got its other wing free, and the lightweight Archie was hanging onto its feet with his arms stretched high whilst rotating on his thin legs like a deranged ballet dancer. It seemed he was about to experience the treat of an aerial view of Clapham and beyond, and the Co-Op staff, doubled up in laughter, cat-called him with their shining gems of facetious advice.

"Talk to 'im nice-like, and let 'im go, Archie. That'll do it..."

"Nah, jump on 'is back, Archie, an' fly 'im 'ome..."

"Wanna bit o' salt to put on his tail?"

And George, himself a character with his continuous patter across the fats counter, stirred at the air with his butter pats and offered his bit of advice.

"Get some string 'round his neck, Archie, and ride 'im 'ome. You can borrow these pats and tap 'im there..."

And there they guffawed and tottered, the Co-Op men, all but helpless in their arcade of fun, pointing out his developing antics and frantically elbow-nudging each other, slapping at their thighs and reaching for their apron hems to dry their streaming eyes, whilst Archie, preoccupied beyond the hearing of their sardonic advice, fought with all his might to hang on to his earnings and his sanity...

When the war came, and Archie's calling-up papers arrived he decided not to bother, so the Military came and took him. He came back on leave a few months later, a fit and clean-shaven soldier who saluted everyone in uniform, even 'bus drivers and cinema commissionaires.

He was soon discharged, though, and took a job as the local road sweeper, and the talk was that Clapham's streets were never better swept. It was with enormous pride that he showed Aunt Nance his first pay-packet.

"Eh, look at this, Nancie... Over two pounds! I 'en't a'doin' so bad, be I?"

"You're doing well." said Aunt Nance. "You want to stick at it, Archie. Make somethin' of yourself." He smiled happily.

"And look what Dorrie Davidson gave me just for sweepin' around the front of her shop, Nancie." he said. And he showed her a bag of unsold cakes.

But as the days slipped by the regular wage and security of his new job failed to compensate him for the timeless and spontaneous life he loved best, and he soon settled back to being Clapham's odd job man.

His 'Pram and Nance's Front

His sense of humour was brief and impish, and it flew in rare and harmless bursts. One day he asked Aunt Nance whether he might leave his old 'pram on her front for a day or so.

"You don't mind, do y'u, Nancie?" he asked.

"Not if it's only for a day or two, Archie." she said. "But no longer, mind. I like to keep my bit o' front tidy." So he left it there, and it lingered for several days, and it wasn't long before the nosily personable Syd Fry came by, coughing politely and looking curious.

"Er... We was wonderin' 'ow things be a workin' out b'tween you an' Archie, Nancie," he ventured.

"Eh?" asked Aunt Nance, spinning round. "Between me and Archie? Whatever do you mean, Syd Fry?"

"Oh, nuthin', nuthin'... Only we've sin his 'pram in your front a bit lately, all night an' all, be the look on it, and, well, you know... We sort o' wondered..."

That did it. Nance, a respectable and prim spinster all her life, had to tell Archie to take his pram away, and never to park it there again, because, as she explained, it was causing talk. And when he'd heard her out he gave her a knowing wink, grinned and nudged her, and raised his eyebrows.

"Well, if folks be a talkin', we might as well make it come true, 'adn't us?" he grinned. "What's y'say we makes a start by me a-takin' y'u to the Cadena dance nex' Sat'dee night? Then a'ter, I'll er... see y'u 'ome, like, an'..."

Aunt Nance stepped back in outraged disbelief, then surveying his twinkling little face of ginger stubble with its smoke-hole of a mouth, she found her face reluctantly slipping to a smile.

"I'll have to consult my diary, Archie," she said, entering into the nonsense. "And see if I can fit you in..."

And chortling with glee Archie skipped off with his 'pram towards Dorothy Davidson's. He liked doing jobs for Dorothy, for as well as being promptly paid there was always the likelihood of the cakes...

<u>Archie and Mrs Garlick</u>

It was whilst working there that he noticed that Mrs Garlick's old shed, across the yards, was tottering, and always on the lookout for his next job, he saw to it that he chanced across her path when she next came out.

"'Ow be y'u, Mrs Garlick." he said. "I always likes to bump into the likes of gennelfolk like you." She looked at him soberly. He smiled at her.

"You looks quite a Lady today, Mrs Garlick."

"You'm kind, Archie."

"I knows class when I sees it, that's all." It was Mrs Garlick's turn to smile.

"Now what is it, Archie?" she asked. "Be you 'ungry?"

"No, nothin' like that, Mrs Garlick... Oney, er... I sees as your shed's a bit rickety. Wants lookin' at, like..."

"I knows it, Archie, I knows it."

"'Er... I'm a'comin' into some nice cakes tomorrah, Mrs Garlick, an' I hopes to bring you a few..."

"Oh, good, Archie. I likes nice cakes, specially when they'm gifts from rich an' 'andsome gennulmen. Now, what time be you a-comin', 'cos I'm a-playin' polo with the Duke o' Gloucester all day, then I'm off to Buck'n'am Palace fer dinner an' dancin' with the King."

Trouble in The Coach and Horses

He'd call at The Coach of an evening, where he'd slide his coins across the bar and bask in the sweet happiness of the brew. He enjoyed his pint - or two or three - at the end of a busy day, and everybody conceded that he'd worked as hard for it as any of the others in the place. But Syd, the landlord, could be a testy cove at times, and one morning Archie recounted to Nance that the night before he'd made to throw him out.

"Syd turned nasty on me last night, Nancie." he said. "When I wen' in I sin as 'e 'ad a few o' Johnnys' big-wigs in, an' 'e come over an' talked to me quiet-like. 'You can get straight out o' 'ere tonight, Archie.' he said, 'Cos I got good company, an' I 'ent 'a goin' to serve y'uh.'"

"I said to 'im 'What d'y'uh mean, Sid?' an' 'e said. 'You 'eard me Archie, so get out.'"

"So I told him straight, Nancie, same as 'e told me. I said 'Look 'ere, Syd Smith. Nobody knows you beller'n I do, an' I remembers as when we was kids you 'ad no backside to y'ur trousers 'alf the time, an' you 'ad to get up the market to pinch a few 'taters fer y'r dinner, an' pinch a drop o' milk from the milkers, just the same as us.'"

"'You oughta've a-sin 'im, Nancie, twisting 'is 'head around an' lookin' over to the big-wigs as 'e'd bin with, an' flappin' 'is 'and behind 'im at me, an' tellin' me to shush...'"

He stood there nodding and reflecting, then looked at Aunt Nance earnestly.

"'E come off of it a'ter that. But fancy 'im tellin' me to get out, Nancie." he said. "I've alwi's bin quiet there. I a'n't never bin no trouble to nobody in a pub, Nancie. You knows that."

There came the time that he had to go to the City General Hospital for a day or two. He smartened himself up for the occasion, and walked briskly to Great Western Road complete with a newly acquired overcoat and trilby and some well-polished shoes. When they discharged him they arranged for his acceptance into a protective hostel where he'd be looked after. But he didn't stick it for long. He soon traded its antiseptic refuge for the spice and freedoms of his Clapham life, with its bits of casual work and his pots of beer at The Coach. The life that nestled in his blood, the only life he'd known…

His Last Winter

But as time slipped on, his loneliness began to tell on him. He saw less to go home to at each day's end, and took to sleeping anywhere. In an old hut here, a barn there, the corner of a shed, and, for a while, in a forgotten war-time 'pill-box' at Highnam. But with each day's dawning he'd be up and about, trotting the streets as ever with his 'pram, to see what the new day held for him.

Eventually he settled in a derelict hovel in St. Catherine's Street, but there came a cold winter and his way of living began to tell on him. He came to look sallow and rough, and thin and frail. Then one day he came struggling past Aunt Nance's house as she was sweeping her front. His 'pram was piled high with logs, and she saw at once that he was scarcely up to pushing it. He looked ill; his eyes were red-rimmed and watery and he was coughing and glinting with sweat.

"Archie, whatever's the matter with you?" she cried. He paused and wiped his brow with his sleeve.

"I feels awful, Nancie," he said.

"Then for God's sake get to your doctor right away." she urged.

"'A'n't got one, Nancie." he replied.

"Well, slip along to the City General" she said. "Here - I'll come with you…" and she put down her brush. But as she made to get her coat he touched her arm, looked down at his 'pram-full of logs and shook his head.

"Nancie, I golla get this lot to Mrs Cooper." he said. "'Er's a-waitin' to get 'er fire a-goin'." And off he went, leaving her looking after him and sadly picking at her lip.

A day or two later Bill, an acquaintance of his, found him collapsed in his hovel, and pulling him onto his old 'pram he ran him to the City General hospital. And there, a day or two later, he died, and an emptier Clapham mourned the loss of one of its richest and best-loved characters.

Chapter 8

Johnny Stephens

Around the corner from the Coach and Horses, just inside the Skinner Street loop, hung the stern gates of 'Johnnys', an enterprise begun by John Stephens in 1870 as a vinegar and pickles factory. He added jams to its range in 1893, and by 1897, when he enlarged it, he had over four hundred employees, most of whom were women.

It had changed little by the 'Thirties. A shanty happening of draughty dens and halls of scarred brick and iron, Johnny's resembled a Dickensian workhouse with its tiny prison-like windows and its patchwork of rough and sundry floors.

The fruits and sugars were boiled and jarred in the main building, which bordered the road; the vinegars and pickles were brewed in a cavernous den behind, and the jars and bottles that would contain them all were washed in buckets of hot water in a cobbled yard under a corrugated roof.

It was a celebrated firm, Johnnys', an institution nationally acclaimed, and to its province of women workers the rhythm of its title was a balm. It was an ancient and decrepit place of whitewash and cobwebs and draughts and primitive conditions, where (until they were granted stools, many years later) the women worked standing on concrete floors. They shivered in winter and baked in summer, and a job there meant an early start to their long and arduous days of closely managed grafting.

But there were compensations. Johnnys' was their spirited haven of shared joys and troubles, the hub of their culture of fellowship, their club. And if their days ran hard there, they did no more than match their lives.

They knew no concept of a welfare state, not even by distant dreams, and with the ongoing unemployment among their menfolk, the Johnnys' pay-packet was often the only one to enter a home. It was the saving of many a Clapham family, Johnny's.

Their 'Piece'

Another bonus - for some at least - came incidentally. Every Johnnys' woman was provided with what was known as their 'piece', a square of sacking which they tied around their waists, like an apron, to protect their clothes. After work they'd fold and roll their 'piece' and take it home under their arm, and many a pot of jam or pickle, or a cabbage or cauliflower found their way into a rolled-up 'piece' for spiriting past the gateman.

But there came the odd mishap. Mrs Wingate's fish and chip shop on the Knapp was just round the corner from Johnny's, and at the end of one lean day our mother gathered up a wad of old newspapers and sent me there with them in the hope that Mrs Wingate would express her thanks with a bag of chips which might make our supper.

The shop was empty but for a few lumpy Johnny's women with their rolled-up 'pieces'. A pot of new and unset jam, secreted in Beryl Gray's 'piece', must have been poorly sealed, for a trail of jam was trickling down her coat. The slow-moving but fast-thinking Mrs Wingate, behind the counter, saw it too, and lighting up her eyes, she chided Beryl wickedly.

"Aw, look, Ber', your pot o' Johnnys' jam 'ave come undone and spoilt y'ur coat. If I was you I'd take it back an' get a new pot out of 'em. An' a new coat, too, whilst you'm at it. Shameful, I calls it. They don't care 'ow they doos the tops of their jam up these days. I 'ouldn't 'ave it, Ber'."

And Beryl stood there shuffling and pulling a watery smile onto her face as fast and repeatedly as her shame kept pulling it off.

The women had another popular way of smuggling their pilfered pots of jam out of Johnnys', and it worked every time, though the part-time gateman, Tom Mahoney, knew all about it.

"I can tell where the buggers stows the jam by the clumsy way they walks a-past me," he'd say. "But what can a fella do about it, eh? What can a fella do? You answer me that 'un!"

93

Gateman Mahoney

Tom Mahoney, the Knapp butcher, arrived at Johnnys' at seven each morning to unlock the gates to let the workers in. Any who arrived before three minutes past he allowed in without penalty. Those who followed before five past would lose fifteen minutes' pay, and any who came later than five past would be sent home until the afternoon start.

A small crowd of unemployed hopefuls always collected at Johnnys' gates in case a casual job or two arose. And as they waited, they gossiped, for 'The Gates' was their garnering post for news of other work.

"I 'ear they'm after a barmaid at the K.A., Liz. (The K.A. was the locals' colloquialism for the King's Arms, at the top of Hare Lane.) 'T'ain't no good for me, o' course, not with the kids, but it might do for you..."

"'Ere, Lil, Ruby Horsham wants a bit o' Sat'd'ee 'elp with the 'taters and veg, like. 'Course, 'er's busy with her flowers on a Sat'd'ee. 'Er's bright an' sharp, mind, but 'er's *ever* so nice.
(Ruby Horsham was a prominent Northgate Street florist.)

"An' they'm after a cleaner at the Lu'e, now as Maisey's bad." Then a slow wink. "Say as you knows Wyndham Lewis."

"They wants another cook at the Spread, Mo., but I can't fit in with th' 'ours, not with me job at the Bon. But you could leave your 'Enry 'is bit o' dinner, couldn't y'u?"

At ten past seven Mahoney would appear again, to hang one of two signs on the gates. If it read 'Hands Wanted' there would be a forward surge and Mahoney would announce his news.

"A morning's work for three women." he might call, and after looking them over he'd select three and allow them in. Then, if appropriate, he'd address the waiting men.

"There's a day's work for one man and a morning's work for another." And many a man past his best would try to look sprightly enough to be chosen. But more often than not the sign would read 'No Hands Wanted' and there'd be a flurry of movement, some

94

hurrying off to look for work elsewhere and others falling into knots to air their hopes or fly their snippets of despair.

I don't suppose Johnnys' part-time gateman enjoyed his hiring power. He wasn't that sort of man. But a critical cynicism reigned amongst the unselected. They held that Mahoney allocated his jobs to those who bought their meat at his butchers'shop.

The Johnny's Smell

The spices of the Empire sailed through Johnnys' gates. And as they mixed and simmered in its silver bowls, the magic of their mingling laced the air, and flew Clapham heady in its scents.

The smell that rose from Johnnys' was unique. It was sweet and bitter and sour and fresh, and root-rank and stark, and blossom-touched. It was as spry as a mayfly, heavy as fermenting wine, as gentle as whimsy, and as capricious as a fleeting thought. On balmy days it came near tangible, almost a meal, a piquant plot of essences that teased the tongue and watered the throat. It grew us our mid-morning pangs, pulled us to our dinner as the sun slid by, and drew us to our supper as our passage grew its shapes. And when we went to bed we breathed it from our sheets.

It floated its seasoning through Clapham, the Johnny's smell, and sowed a flavour foreign, yet its own. It hung in our hair, flavoured our furnishings, and hid in the clothes we wore. It was the scent of a lifetime, a chest of sensuous treasure, an aromatic compendium that once tasted, would lie in the blood forever, never to stray or to fade. It was a friend, that smell, and it is with me now.

I Meet Algie

About this time I met Algie. He had a new old bike, and we were taking it in turns to pedal it around the Knapp when we noticed the Knapp Cafe's cat dozing on its paves. Its tail was outstretched, and the devil slipped to us... It was Algie's turn, and after we'd whispered together he rode energetically towards the cat

95

and pounced on his saddle as his wheel hit its tail. The result surpassed our hopes. The cat issued a scream that hit the houses, threw itself up the wall as though possessed, and bounced around the Knapp like a shell.

Our delight was intense. We sank in our wicked laughter and flew lost in our joy. And as our tears cleared we looked about and saw Wadley's tom. It was my turn. I aimed the bike, drove it like a rocket, and caught its tail well, leaping and thudding on the saddle as I scored. That cat gave us a good show, too, and shot away forever.

We had found a new game, and we played it out. Cats sat everywhere, and fell readily to us, but after a while those that remained tended to sit with their tales wrapped close. But we found an answer. Whilst Algie hung ready on the bike, I would befriend the victim-to-be, and stroke and pamper it until it trusted me. Then I'd gently stretch out its tail, give Algie the nod, and jump back as he thundered up. And next time, I'd ride the bike. It always worked.

We had caught just about every cat in the district - some more than once - when we were spotted by the passing Reverend Harwood, of St. Mark's, who gently extracted our promises to stop it. And even then, we got a few more, during the early evenings, when his church organ swelled.

Spider Killing

Nor was that the full extent of our wickedness. The next morning, when the Knapp was at its busiest, with the brewers' draymen roping their barrels down to the pub cellars, the delivery wagons and carts discharging their wares to the shops, and with everybody about their business, Algie came over.

"I knows how to kill spiders." he said, and as I absorbed this news he offered more. "These daddy longlegs is best. When I kills 'em, their legs keeps a'goin', even when I pulls 'em off and puts 'em in this matchbox."

We looked into our passage and found a spider, a fawn-coloured gangling thing with a set of long legs that danced from its pellet of a head. He held it on the passage step, pulled a three-inch nail from his pocket and drove its point into the spider's head. Its legs kicked madly, and we picked them from their yellow pulp and put them, still kicking, into the matchbox.

"There's lots more o' these in your passage." said Algie.

"Let's kill 'em, all, then." I said, and we reaped them in and merrily settled to their slaughter. Then I got an idea.

"Let's use the flat end of the nail." I said. "It just fits their heads."

"Oh-ah!" enthused Algie, so we drove their brains out that way, and they kicked even better, and we soon had a step rich in crushed head pulp and a boxful of madly twitching legs. Just then our mother came out of our passage and slipped past us and into the butchers'. Algie and I whispered together, and when she came smiling back, I handed her the matchbox.

"For you, Mam." I said. She smiled indulgently, popped her newspaper parcel under her arm, gently took the box, and, preparing to slide it open, smiled at us again.

"Go on, open it, Mam." I said. She widened her smile, dropped her chin, and entering into our world, held the box close to her face and pushed out the tray.

Immediate chaos broke. She issued a shock of piercing screams and flung it into the air. Out ran Mahoney with a leg of pork in one hand and a cleaver in the other and Mrs Wingate, flying from her shop, demolished her queue of several lumpy women. And as the kicking legs fell all over our mother she frantically galloped everywhere and anywhere, tugging at her clothes, pawing at her hair, and bucking like a stampeding colt.

The Knapp's population flew petrified and silenced at her sudden apparent possession. Then one or two kind people, finding movement, ran over and soothed her, and brushed off some of the legs, and sat her on our pulpy step and comforted her, whilst Algie and me, draped in her sausages and chops, stood hooting and wheezing and clutching at each other for support until our eyes streamed and our sides ached.

Only later did we pay the price...

Chapter 9

All Good Things...

From soon after its earliest days, Clapham, with its sea of chimney pots, its self-contained society of unskilled men, and its powerful community spirit, attracted the brewers. They knew that the less money folk could gather together for their long-term aspirations, the more they'd spend buying their day-to-day pleasures. And because it was a man's world the pubs rose thick in Clapham. I remember The White Lion, The Magnet, The Anchor, The Pheasant, The Rose and Crown, The Duke of York, and the two Suffolks - The Inn and The Arms. The Kingsholm Inn and The Fortune of War stood together in Kingsholm Road, just round Sweetbriar Street's corner, The White Hart was a bit further along, and nearby, on the Knapp, were The Coach and Horses, The Rose and Crown and The Worcester Arms. Most were beer houses only –'Licensed to sell beer and porter' read the signs over their doors.

Pub Fights

Their reputations varied, and some came rough at times, especially on Saturday nights. Notable among them was The Magnet, a beer-swimming den on the corner of Suffolk Street and Union Street, which was used by the gipsies as well as local Clapham folk, and noted for the ferocity of its weekend fights, which often spilled into the street. Betty Redburn, who lived with her family over their Columbia Street shop, found them exhilarating when she was a little girl.

"The fights were *spectacular* at times" she told me. "Especially those between Wally and Violet Gough, a local married couple. When my people put me to bed on Saturday nights, I used to make my dad promise to come up and wake me if the Goughs started their fights, so that I could watch them from my window over the shop, which looked out over the pub. And he did, and I loved it! They were really something, those fights..."

The Fortune of War, in Kingsholm Road, just around the corner from Sweetbriar Street and next door to The Kingsholm Inn, was almost monopolised by the gipsy clans, and even more notorious for its fights than The Magnet. It was an old-fashioned horse-trading post with a stabling yard, and a colony of itinerant horse dealers had long since made it their own, stabling their animals there for their Saturday horse fairs.

They ran their horses up and down the Kingsholm Road and did their trading in the yard, and colourful and crowded affairs the sales were, too, with casual dealers and fortune tellers and cardsharps meshing with the rogues and tricksters and the sots. And as the drink flowed and the blushing sun roamed towards the Forest, there often rose bickerings that shot to bouts of fisticuffs, and Clapham's well-known pugilists, the Weavers, the Burfords, the Bowens, and the Mountfords, stepped to the fore.

They'd fight off the outsiders, these merry men, then fight amongst themselves for recreation. Then they'd come tired, patch up their grievances, buy each other drinks and swap their yarns until the pubs disgorged them. And clinging and swaying together they'd sing themselves off homewards, their trailing voices cracked, their timing gone and the words of their songs all awry. And Clapham's moderate folks of temperance, tucked in their snug and cosy beds, would lift their heads and smile, and drink in their conviviality, and slip to their sleep well cheered with the flavours of the Clapham that they loved.

Escape of the Cinemas

But another means of escape had come to challenge the pubs. Talking pictures had burst to the Bowl, and the exotically named Theatre de Luxe, Clapham's local world of celluloid, had sprung the first to show them. And for coppers, too. It was all too good to miss...

So, when their bit of money ran to it, off to the Lu'e they trooped, the kindled souls of Clapham, to span the world from their cosy seats, in the Hollywood company of Gable and Garbo, and Harlow and Beery and the rest, all so essentially enmeshed in their synthetic plights...

I remember the day that Granny Boden traded her kitchen and scooped me up for a spell at the Lu'e. She'd seen Grampy Boden off in search of work, then called to collect me.

"Y'ur dad's gone t' the foundry, Flor." she told my mother. "Didn't want to, mind, but I kept on to 'im 'cos Phyllis Edge reckoned as they wanted four men fer 'alf a day. God knows we could do with the bit o' money. Any'ow, we'd beller get off t' the Lu'e. Come on then, Donny." And off we went, to a tall and vast carpet-cosseted world of glow-worm lights and silent isolation from the world. I can still remember my elation. It was the first time I'd walked on carpet, or been under electric lights. Girls with twinkling stars took us to our seats and we looked to a wall of golden drapes that seemed to hang from the heavens.

The lights dimmed, the flickering stars danced away, and a thunderous melody soared as the cinema's manager, the white suited and spotlighted Wyndam Lewis, seated at the giant Wurlitzer organ, came gliding to the centre-stage in a pool of gently changing pastel hues that sent him primrose yellow, then powder blue, then lime green, then pink...

He sailed us a series of bright and spirited and familiar melodies, songs of echoes in the valleys, lilacs in the spring, poppies blooming again, and blushing sails in warm and sleepy sunset seas.

And, when he'd sowed his melodies and sailed away, Hollywood's magic lantern came crinkling at the drapes, and they glided open by unseen hands to show us a world of wonder that took our breath away...

We saw an outback homestead on a road of dust, with its tumble of shops and its unlikely looking bank, and spied a hard faced outlaw watching a happy couple strolling hand in hand. As yet there was no shooting, and after some fidgeting I looked up at

Granny Boden. She had slipped lost, and found herself in the film's dreams...

She smiled as the happy couple played, lowed and hissed as the villain struck, stiffened as the conflicts grew, fumbled for her hanky as the heroine wept, and hummed her relief when the villain met his end. And as the music swelled and the hero found his love, she looked up sweetly from her lowered face, and I saw, for a moment, not my ravaged Gran but the sweet face of 'Nellie' - Ellen, her youngest daughter.

The curtains swished the film away and we emerged, me to the cold blue light and the cuffing breeze of reality, and Granny Boden to her rose-coloured and sweet-scented dreams. I looked at her. Her worn face had found peace, and slipped settled and wistful. She'd come lifted, and walked with a lighter step, as though still in that softer world of purity, romance, and happy endings...

Then she looked down at me, caught my eyes on hers, and smiled and rucked my hair.

"Nice picture, wa'n't it, Donnie." she said as she pulled my collar up against the breeze. "'E was a nasty devil, mind, but 'e got 'is come-uppance in th' end. An' so they should, too, all the buggers." And she gripped my hand and we quickened our pace towards home.

"I'm 'ungry, Donnie, ain't you?" she said. "I could do with summat to eat – like some nice fish 'n' chips. Let's see if your Grampy found that work an' brought us a bit o' money 'ome..."

The Reverend Harwood

The folk of Clapham were a down to earth and pragmatic people alright, but their values were sound, and one man was universally respected. The Reverend Robert Harwood, the vicar of their St. Mark's Church was loved by all, believers and non-believers alike. A common site as he walked the Clapham streets in his black cloak, his pink and alert face radiated an infectious aura of sunny serenity and affection for all, as well as his contentment with his flock. A perceptive, kindly man, he had a smile and a cheery word for all, especially when he sensed that a person was ill at ease.

Folks knew that as long as their vicar was there, they were not alone. 'I wonder what the Reverend would think?' was a common utterance where a problem arose, and he could be depended upon to listen attentively. And the children, even the roughnecks, revered him. And his interests weren't merely spiritual; he helped folk practically, and sailed on his sunny way as they foundered him their thanks.

I recall the time that I had an early morning paper round, which entailed my delivering papers to the plethora of ancient and restful little dwellings in the cathedral grounds, to the booming music of its bells. Suddenly I was greeted by the sunny Reverend, who came sweeping by at his usual purposeful pace. He paused and smilingly asked me whether I had almost finished my deliveries.

"Not many more, Reverend." I replied, and his pink face broke into a comforting smile.

"Not many more..." he echoed, perhaps reflecting upon the optimism of the young, and rucking my hair with his hand he swept on his way.

He had a sense of humour, too, and was quite without arrogance. One cold morning, when we children were waiting outside Redburns' shop for our Open Air School 'bus, the Reverend came sailing along the opposite pavement, towards his church. It was April Fools' Day, and Rags Collins, an older boy among us, mooted the idea of playing a prank on the Reverend.

"Let's get 'im goin' - come on..."

"We mustn't – 'e's the Reverend..."

"Aw, come on..."

"Naw, not the Reverend... 'Ouldn't be right... 'Ouldn't be respectful..."

But Rags was determined. After the usual greeting and cheery word, the Reverend made to continue, and Rags called over to him:

"Reverend, your cloak is torn!" The Reverend stopped, registered his surprise and reeled round on his toes as he tried to find the damage in his swirling cloak. Then he heard the laughter and spun round, clearly nonplussed.

"April Fool, sir!" called Rags, and the Reverend, realising the date, broke into a warm and ready smile.

"Of course!" he said. "It's April the first! You certainly caught me that time, you rascals!" And with his smile now a laugh of delight, he sailed on with renewed vigour, clearly delighted at his close affinity with the up and coming fabric of Clapham. And the urchins were no less contented with their Reverend.

Demolition of Clapham

But all good things come to an end, and so it was to be with the haven that was Clapham. To destroy a culture, runs the adage, you first destroy its habitat. And that's precisely what happened in the 'Fifties, in the name of Progress.

The council's faceless men didn't see Clapham as it was - a golden community of kindred folk, a city of plucky and interdependent souls with their own civilisation with its simple and spontaneous welfare scheme, a parish that had thrived for well over a century, not on pretensions but on the joyful living of its lives; a magical culture within a culture.

They saw only a stretching huddle of wayward dens that knew no order and begged no rules of symmetry, a mess of dwellings far removed from their modern concept of neat and orderly and sterile rows of pale brick boxes on concrete roads... And they fell disturbed.

"Something must be done!" they cried, and their bright and brand new protégées came measuring the buildings and counting their scars, and testing their goodness against their modern lists. Then they sadly shook their heads, and deemed Clapham bad.

"These people need our help," they said, and they set about destroying them. Nobody asked them whether they wanted their ancient culture ravaged, whether they wanted its sturdy humanity uprooted and dispersed to unknown and rootless localities with which they knew no affinity. They blithely insisted - as do-gooders do - that they knew best. That the folks of Clapham would be better off living in cold and distant boxes in churned and lumpy fields remote from anywhere.

Their reckless and wicked folly began in 1956 and ran into 1957, and I can still hear the thudding bulldozers and the chugging lorries. Still see the rubble. Still taste the heavy dust of Clapham's end.

First, they razed Sweetbriar Street, its backbone, and its foundry. Then they flattened Sherbourne Street, Union Street, and Suffolk Street. Then they finished off the north-eastern side of Alvin Street, already half-ravaged by the demolition of its side streets. Then Sweetbriar Street's three little cul-de-sacs, Guinea, Worrall and Counsel Streets, the last two of which had been proudly named after George Worrall Counsel, Clapham's creator.

Alec Redburn's Shop

That left only Columbia Street, and they trundled their bulldozers there and set about completing their destruction. But as they razed their way towards Alec Redburn's shop they encountered a problem. He refused to move.

"I've spent my life in this little place of mine," he said. "And I'm staying here. I'm too old to start again."

Undaunted for the moment, the bulldozers attacked the houses each side of Alec's, and when they'd done, his shop stood alone in the dry prairie of dust and rubble that had been Clapham. One of a terrace row, its sides now displayed the wallpapered walls of its former neighbours beneath the edges of its splintered roof. They had reduced his shop a lone ruin. But still he refused to leave, and in case it fell in on him whilst their intimidation continued, they tidied the damaged edges of its roof and bricked up its exposed sides.

I called upon Alec at that time and found the shop a desolate and dusty shell, yet he still had a few greens on display on the bit of pavement they had left him. And Alec, ravaged but as dapper as ever, was still dancing about the place, moving an empty box from here, a hollow crate to there, a few cleared sweet jars to this shelf, some caved-in cartons to that... Then turning to his counter he tidied his ledger, laid his bit of pencil beside it, wafted the dust from his cutting board and knives, and resettled his sheets of greaseproof paper.

I looked at him. He was keeping everything up-together for the parish of customers he would never see again. And all the time he was humming a tuneless and urgent and endless tune...

He had spent his top-gear life serving his customers right in that shop, and, because his brain had grown tuned to it, he still busied himself there. It had been his family home, and living, for forty years, and his heart clung to it as though it was his very life. And in truth it was his life. He knew no other.

They sent their friendly and silver-tongued men to try to change his mind, and followed them with their loud and not so friendly men with their papers. Then they sent him their letters, first advising, then demanding, and then threatening him. Then the bullies came thumping at his door. But Alec remained firm.

"My shop's been my life," he said. "And it's still my life. To move from here would be the end of me."

At ten o'clock the following morning they called upon Alec's daughter, Betty, at her wool shop in nearby Worcester Street.

"We've demolished Clapham but for your father's shop." they told her. "Now that's got to come down too. Our bulldozer is running beside it, waiting to start. We're asking you to come with us to get him to leave. Will you do that?"

"I'll come and ask him to leave." replied Betty, reaching for her coat. "But I doubt if he will, because he knows – just as we know - that it would be the end of him."

So she went there, as they asked, and clambered over the rubble to his shop, the family home of her childhood and beyond, where she found him as I had left him, tidying his shelves and brushing at the dust. But now he was silently weeping. And as she tearfully begged him to leave, the bulldozer dealt the house a blow that shook it in its roots. Then another, and yet another... And as the ceiling began to rain its debris, Alec's spirit foundered and he allowed his daughter to lead him out.

"When we shuffled through that door, I looked at his face through my tears." Betty told me. "And I saw only the shadow of the Dad I'd known. He was a shell of a man without hope. He was finished." She fell silent, and I waited...

"He seemed so frail, and so small." she said. "And I could see he'd lost his will to live. He'd left it in the shop that was his life. It was the end of him, and the end of our mother too. He soon died of a broken heart, and without him by her side, so did she."

The End of Clapham

So with Alec's shop gone, that was the end of the bricks and mortar Clapham. The houses, the shops, the school, the pubs, the streets...

But what of its people - its culture of folks who'd lived there all their lives, like their people before them, for over a century and a quarter?

They discarded them, the faceless men. Split them up and tossed them to a mess of distant and soulless nowheres, and left them isolated and broken in their sterile and alien boxes. And robbed of the warmth of their sustaining community, the old folks pined in their isolation for the only life they'd ever known or wanted, the only life that they'd been taught to live.

And many of them lost their wills to live, and they too died in their hordes - of broken hearts. All cruelly and judicially murdered by the kind and caring city fathers.

That Happy Breed

So with Clapham destroyed, razed to the ground by a band of wanton and misguided do-gooders and well-wishers, what can be said about the wonderful and happy breed that it had sustained for so long?

That the folks of Clapham were the salt of the earth. That they were a highly moral and law abiding people who spent their golden days in peaceful contentment, where kindness towards each other was endemic, where nobody was lonely, where the spry helped the lame and where everybody belonged. Where folks passing through were sheltered for the night, where passing tramps were received with simple humanity and hospitality and sent on their way with their tea cans filled and with food in their bellies. Where the streets rang with the happy banter of its playing children, and where the likes of the old and blind and crippled Mr Priest could be sure of a cheery word as he shuffled and tapped his way about.

A society that never knew locked doors, scarcely saw a policeman, whose roughneck youths stopped their horseplay as old folks came past, and where their church and vicar were revered. A society of good and guileless people whose communal spirit flowed like nectar and who wore their poverty like garlands.

Gone for good. Wantonly destroyed. And a shamed Gloucester will never see its like again.

Would that we could aspire to such a society today in this corner of this once sceptered isle. Sadly, we can't. But those who are left still have the treasure of their Clapham memories. And thankfully, the vandals can't ravage them.

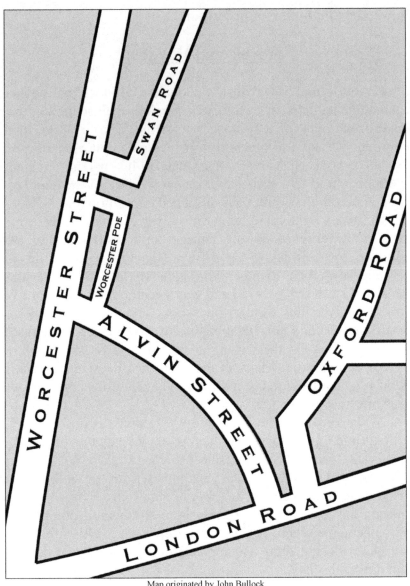

Map originated by John Bullock
'All good things…'

In preparation by the same author...

<u>Hovels and Haydust</u>

Hovels and Haydust, Donald Bullock's boyhood autobiography, tells two stories in parallel against the colourful social background of the Gloucester of the 'Thirties. That of the unfurling life and adventures of a perceptive Gloucester boy born into its central backstreets, and that of his parents' romantic determination to find their happiness in the face of the depression and of their families' bitter and sustained opposition.

He writes lightly and humorously, yet with telling realism, of how, in the absence of any concept of a welfare state, folks depended, for their day-to-day survival, upon their own efforts and the support of their friends and neighbours, and of the resulting communal spirit that evolved and was a central factor in their lives. How the adversities of the times both brought out the best in people and bred a proliferation of local characters and rascals driven to living on their wits, so providing a backcloth of rich intrigue and humour. Many of the characters he identifies are, by today's standards, scarcely credible, and he describes them all with an astonishing perception.

At the age of six he found himself trading his day-to-day life in the grime of the backstreet hovels for the haydust of the open countryside, when he was selected for a place at Oakbank. Oakbank was an 'Open Air School' set in the rolling local countryside and opened as the pilot of a new and forward-thinking concept, for those likely to benefit from its tranquil setting and its sympathetic approach. It was the turning point of his life, and he emerged with an affinity and appreciation of the countryside that is with him to this day.

In Hovels and Haydust he tells of 'slipping into his life' in a mahogany drawer on the flagstones of a cottage yard, and takes the reader to the many places he called home in those early 'faded days' of the 'Thirties. He describes, in his memorable and captivating prose, the 'tiny, earthy and parochial' pre-war market town of Gloucester with its central, street-soiling cattle-market life and its host of characters, of the parcel-carrying days of he and his peers at its ornate railway stations and its busy Westgate Street 'bus centre, of the 'Roses and Thorns' his Knapp days, his idyllic Oakbank life, and his desperately unhappy years at the notoriously cruel and sadistic London Road National School. His description and incidental analysis of his teachers, particularly those of the heinous National School, is a lesson in both the brilliant perception of a child's mind and the power of the written word.

He tells, too, of his grandparents. Of Granny Boden, the kindly, hopeless soul who devoted her short life to the up-bringing of her crop of five daughters and of her husband, the charismatic and mysterious Grampy Boden, a proud and laconic man who nursed two identities; of the cold, scheming and manipulative witch that was his Grandma Bullock, and of her quietly diminutive and easily managed husband, Grampy Bullock.

Hovels and Haydust is more than an account of a city boy's life in the 'Thirties. It is a perceptively drawn together social document of the times in the tiny and parochial Gloucester of the day.

Now in its final preparation, Hovels and Haydust will be compulsive reading for those who knew the charm of the Gloucester of the 'Thirties, for those who are part of the Gloucester of today, and those who relish a well-told human story of hopes and aspirations, joys, tragedies and disillusionments. The book is told against a backcloth of rich and telling humour and set in the earthily charming, invigorating and bustling Gloucester that has long since gone for ever, never to return...

Hovels and Haydust, by Donald Bullock, will be published by the Wheatley Press.

The Wheatley Press
Innsworth Technology Park, D5
Innsworth Lane
Gloucester, GL3 1DL
England.

www.wheatleypress.com

INDEX

iv

Printed in Great Britain
by Amazon

28476553R10079